The SECRETS *of* CREATING CUSTOMERS *for* LIFE

Dr. Richard Kaye

October 2017

Fifth House Publishing
1335 Paseo del Pueblo Sur - 268
Taos, New Mexico 872571

For information on distribution rights, royalties, derivative
works, or licensing opportunities on behalf of this content or
work, please contact Dr. Richard Kaye via email at
rkaye@richardkaye.com

COMPANIES, ORGANIZATIONS, INSTITUTIONS,
AND INDUSTRY PUBLICATIONS: Quantity discounts
are available on bulk purchases of this book for reselling,
educational purposes, subscription incentives, gifts,
sponsorship, or fund raising. Special books or book excerpts
can also be created to fit specific needs such as private labeling
with your logo on the cover and a message from a VIP printed
inside. Contact Dr. Kaye at rkaye@richardkaye.com

Library of Congress Cataloging-in-Production Data
10 9 8 7 9 5 4 3 2

Kaye, Richard
The Secrets of Creating Customers for Life: Developing the
strategies, skills, and knowledge to enhance your customers'
experience, creating more business, resulting in more wealth
in your life so you can take better care of yourself and your
family.

Manufactured in the United States of America

ISBN 978-0-692-94463-9   2017913665

More praise from readers of
The Secrets of Creating Customers for Life

"Richard has taken some complex concepts, and through stories, makes them all so easy to understand, and, more importantly, implement. This book is rich with information; however, unless you implement, all you'll have is another book for your library. If you take only ten percent of what will learn in this book and put it into play, your business will grow."
— David E. Stanley, writer, film producer, founder of Impello Entertainment

"*The Secrets of Creating Customers for Life* is a great down and dirty business training course that gives people the actionable steps to take in order to win at the game of business. I liked the homespun nature of the stories. It felt like I was meeting your neighbors and friends."
— Aaron Young, CEO Laughlin Associates

"Richard Kaye is a masterful communicator and a by product of his talent is that he's known for his incredible closing skills. And many will attest that closing is right up there with oxygen. Whether you have an hour or ten minutes to spare, *The Secrets Of Creating Customers For Life* will put you ahead of the competition."
— Michelle Anton, TV Producer, Author

"If you've been in business for 20 years or you are just starting out, this is a comprehensive guide to retaining customers for life filled with examples as well as how to! Don't read it like a book. Read it as a guide. Pick the section you need and implement it. Then come back for more. Watch your business grow as a result."

— Leslie Knight
CEO Space Executive Director of Staff

"Richard's book contains much needed business wisdom on marketing; the oldies but goodies, which he weaves with fresh ideas in a nuts and bolts practical approach, are so refreshing to be reminded of time and again, simply because they work. It was an enjoyable read with lots of examples which made it easy to apply to any business, including my own, which is in the field of personal development through body, mind and spirit well being. Richard has a wealth of knowledge to share in marketing, and his book is an excellent addition to any new, growing, or older business wanting to keep a competitive edge with fresh eyes and be reminded of what's important and necessary to do to keep a business thriving."

— Dr. Judy Scher, Director,
Scher Center for Well Being

"This is very accurate, concise, and precise content. I've seen Richard empower, support, and enrich many entrepreneurs through the years (including me!). His experience is invaluable."

— Dame DC Cordova,
CEO Excellerated Business Schools®
Money & You®

This book is dedicated to
you, if you will actually
put into play the
things you'll learn in this book.

Contents

Preface

This book is not about making you rich; it is not a get rich quick scheme.

This book is about wealth accumulation. This book is an amalgamation of proven principles and systems to help you transform your business, no matter what it is: a professional with a practice, a seminar leader, a public speaker, a retail store, a service provider, a coach, a mentor, or almost any other business on the planet.

My experience, from my first career as an electronics engineer, my 30 years practicing chiropractic, my experience as a business growth specialist, and as a public speaker, is that while most of us are really good at our craft or trade, we never learned how to do the business of the business.

When I graduated with my doctorate of chiropractic, and moved from New York to San Diego to establish my practice, we, the graduating class, were, in essence told, "Get your first patient well; they'll refer everyone they know to you." I am now retired over ten years, and still waiting for my patients to refer *everyone* they know. Oh, of course, many of them did refer friends, colleagues, and family members, and that is a great way to grow any practice or any business.

I graduated from chiropractic college in the '70s, and if anyone then understood the concept of turning your patients or clients into raving fans, certainly no one shared that knowledge with me. It was during my decades of practicing as a doctor, as a business growth specialist, and as a public speaker, that I gathered the skills and strategies so essential to creating repeat business; turning your customers into clients and then into raving fans, so you can accumulate wealth, as distinct from cash flow.

If you look in the dictionary, or on the Internet, you'll find the word "customer" is used interchangeably with the word "client." I make a distinction here, based on my several decades of being in business. In my experience, a customer is someone who comes into your store, shop, or consumes your service, as a onetime event. This could be someone just passing through town, or, someone who may have stopped in your restaurant, and neither the owner nor customer expect a repeat visit. And yet, that customer certainly has the ability to refer their friends, family, and colleagues. However, most businesses never follow the protocols in this book, where you can transform what would appear to be a one-time visit into a stream of referrals and enhanced revenue. Near the end of this book, I will present you with data showing you what repeat business and referrals can do to increase your wealth.

Jennifer and Randy own Gutiz (pronounced: goo tease), one of my favorite restaurants here in Taos, New Mexico, where I live. One day, Jennifer asked me to make a comment about their restaurant on the website Trip Advisor. A very smart move. However, what if she had asked for my e-mail address, and the e-mail addresses of every guest, to keep us all apprised of what they're up to; a guest sign in and comment book would do the trick. We're a tourist community here, in Taos, and while the locals often frequent Gutiz, and take our out of town guests there, if they were to implement some of the strategies in this book, Gutiz would generate even more revenue.

Another friend of mine, Kimberly, owns another of my favorite restaurants, Cafe Renato. (I've been told we have about 100 restaurants and other eating establishments, including taco stands, here, in a town of 5,000 people!) Cafe

Renato has won several awards, including an acknowledgment from *Frommer's*, as a "must" when visiting Taos. I suggested she put a sign out front, acknowledging the awards she has won. If you're walking up the street and see two restaurants, one with signage showing the awards they've won and one without such accolades, and you're like most of us, you are more inclined to go to the award-winning place. The principle is true for restaurants, as well as all other businesses, including yours.

I purchased a clothing washer and dryer from D&S Appliance, here, in town. They may view this as a onetime purchase. However, what if they had taken a video testimonial about how thrilled I was with their service, and put it on their website. Had they asked, I would've gladly given them a testimonial. And what if they gather the e-mail addresses of their clients, and send out a monthly newsletter about keeping appliances working properly? Later, I'll talk about such things as a vehicle to grow business; it's called, TOMA (Top of Mind Awareness). The practice of TOMA is effective in a small town like Taos, where D&S is the only appliance store (other than a Sears outlet), or in a place like San

Diego, a county with a population of over three million people, and myriad appliance stores. One of the objects of this book is for you to discover new, as well as some old ways, to ethically and honestly generate more business, which leads to more revenue, which allows you to take better care of yourself and your family.

Leverage what you learn here. This book has so many tools, systems, and strategies, if you implement only a few of them, there is a high probability you will increase your income.

Develop a strategic advantage; you will outperform other businesses, and improve the quality of your life.

Introduction

If someone could wave a magic wand and change something about your chosen profession or business, what one thing would you change?

Would you want an easier way to contact more, better-qualified prospects? Would you want those prospects, as well as your current customers, to view you as even more of a professional, or maybe even more of an "expert" than you are now, in your field?

You may be good now, but how would you like to be even better at making more effective, more persuasive presentations? Perhaps you would like to be more effective at closing sales or handling objections. Or, is repeat business more important to you?

What if your current customers felt you were the only person, or the only business, who understood and could effectively serve their specialized, unique, and individual needs?

Or, how about referrals? Think of the best customer or client you have right now. How would you like to have more people just like them? What one thing would you change to make you a better, happier, more productive, and potentially wealthier, businessperson?

In the chapters to follow, I'll be discussing not only these areas, but other factors that are critical for you to realize more business success. Throughout the pages of this book we'll explore some of the most effective ideas and field-proven methods and techniques you can begin to put to use immediately, to help you increase your sales, improve your business, overcome some of your most difficult problems and challenges, enjoy extra income, have more free time, and find a renewed enjoyment from your chosen business.

Bold statements? You bet.

Read on and discover how I can make such audacious statements.

Hint: Because the stuff in this book really works!

Increasing Your Effectiveness

You know things are changing today, faster and faster and faster than ever before. Technology has become more sophisticated, competition keener, and consumers, the people who buy your products and services, have become more educated and aware.

Your customers or clients have more choices, not only in similar products and services from different companies, but also among the individual people with whom they deal. The more skillful and professional you are at meeting your customers' needs, the bigger advantage you can command, and the more effective and successful you can become.

If you are really going to be effective and successful in the marketplace today, it is necessary, even vital, for you to continually change, improve, adjust, and update your selling, service, and problem solving skills, as well as your methods of marketing and general business operation. It has been said, (and you have no doubt heard) that:

> *"People don't care how much you know, until they know how much you care."*

One of the most effective ways you can show your prospects and customers you care is by helping them solve their problems in a satisfactory, cost-effective, and professional manner.

You will find an "educated client" is one who trusts you and feels comfortable going forward in transactions with you.

Exposure to New Ideas

That's what this program is all about. This book is written with the goal of helping you become the best you can be in a competitive marketplace. It is all about professionalism. My primary goal is for you to be the "consummate professional," a professional who can be trusted.

My secondary goal is to help you become better positioned, so you are more memorable and well-known in your market, which will assist you in exponentially growing your business.

Naturally, this program doesn't claim, nor does it pretend, to have all the answers to all your business problems. No book, course, or seminar could do that.

Rather, the objective of this program is to expose you to some tried, tested, and field-proven ideas, concepts, and techniques that have worked for other business people.

Once acquainted with new information and ideas, it is up to you to decide which ideas can best be tailored to your personal business situation, and how you will begin to use them to better serve your prospects and clients.

Of the myriad topics covered in the workshops and seminars I facilitate are concrete examples of how to be present with people; not just your clients, but everyone in your life. These skills enhance one-on-one relationships, so the other person really knows you are 100 percent present. The workshops are not just lectures (how boring), but interactive and role-playing, so you really get it; you go home not just thinking you got it, but owning it.

This program is not designed to make you a marketing expert, but rather to provide you with the tools the experts, who are already successful in business, are currently using.

Together, we will explore specific marketing, sales, customer service, and business-building techniques others have used to significantly increase their businesses and incomes, with very little extra effort.

You will find many of these ideas easy to implement, and you'll be able to begin using them right away. Others may take a little longer to put in place. Still, others may not be right for you or your operation at all. That's okay. It's not possible to provide 100 percent usable ideas for every person, in every situation.

If you get just one or two good, usable ideas you can put into your business operation that make a difference, your time, effort, and money will be well invested.

How We Retain Information

Getting a new idea is one thing, but what you do with it is even more important than getting it in the first place. Studies on retention show that you remember:

- 10% of what you read
- 22% of what you hear
- 37% of what you see
- 56% of what you see and hear, and up to
- 86% of what you see, hear and do.

So, an idea that is heard but not acted on is about 75 percent less likely to be retained than an idea which is actually put into practice. Turn that around: When you see, hear, and actually *do* something, by implementing a new idea, you have a 75 percent probability of retaining it.

With this realization in mind, it is important to understand that if the information presented in this book is to be of any real value to you, it must not only be read, it must be applied. Which is to say, it must be experienced or acted upon. That means it's going to take some effort on your part.

Concerned about adding new things to your

repertoire? Perhaps you may wish to follow the advice the White Queen (in Lewis Carrol's, *Through the Looking Glass*) offered to Alice when she said, "Why, sometimes I've believed as many as six impossible things before breakfast." She counsels Alice to practice the same skill: believe in the impossible.

In their book, *The Knowing-Doing Gap*, authors, Jeffrey Pheffer and Robert L. Sutton, report that every year there are 1,700 new business books published, $60 billion spent on training, $43 billion spent on consultants, and our universities turn out 80,000 graduates with MBA's. Yet, most businesses continue to operate day in and day out in much the same ways as they've always done. Despite all of that investment, most don't take the extra step of implementing, so nothing changes!

This is just one of the reasons we do interactive training at the workshops.

You see, knowledge without action is no better than no knowledge at all. Just knowing isn't enough. You have to do something with what you know.

The ideas presented in this book work. They're not theory. They're not speculation on what "should" work. They're not philosophical musings. These ideas, concepts, and techniques, are currently in use by business owners across the country. They are being proven in actual field use, day in and day out.

They work for others, and they can work for you. But, you are going to have to take the time to study them, understand them, and make the necessary modifications to tailor them to your own personal and business style and operation. And then finally, you're going to have to apply them to your business.

As a core component of the workshops I present, you participate in exercises to anchor and begin to implement the new material you are exposed to, so when you leave, you can be in the 86 percent retention range. This is much better than just hearing it.

> *"Tell me and I forget. Teach me and I remember.*
> *Involve me and I learn."*
>
> – Benjamin Franklin

Five Steps of Learning and Retention

Learning, the acquisition of new informa-tion or knowledge, and retention, the ability to capture that information and recall it when wanted or needed, is a five-step process:

Impact – Step one. That is, actually embedding the idea in your mind. This embedding can be in the form of a word, a visual observation, or a concept. It makes no difference. Your mind cannot make a distinction between a synthetic or an actual experience. Nor is your mind capable of determining the difference between a conscious or an unconscious impact an idea may have on you. As far as your mind is concerned, those experiences are all the same, and your mind will accept them, regardless of the source.

If information, or an experience, appears real to your mind, your emotions and nervous system respond as though it is real.

Visualization is what I'm talking about, and while it is often used in sports, it can also be used by you for powerful results in virtually any aspect of your life.

The subconscious mind is remarkably powerful, just as powerful as actually doing the thing you are programming into your subconscious mind.

"Not only does a visualized experience condition the human brain," says Judd Blaslotto, Ph.D., a world-class powerlifter and author of several books on mind control, "but it will also program the human body."

With proper visualization, you can accomplish amazing things.

At the University of Chicago, a study was conducted to determine the effects of visualization on the free-throw performance of basketball players.

Athletes were tested to determine their free-throw proficiency, then randomly assigned to one of three experimental groups.

One group went to the gym every day for an hour to practice throwing free throws.

The second group simply visualized themselves throwing free throws.

The third group did nothing.

After 30 days, the three groups were again tested to determine their free-throw proficiency.

The third group, as would be expected, turned in lower scores.

The first group improved their scores by 24 percent.

The second group, the group that "only" used visualization, tuned in improved scores of 23 percent!

Twenty-three percent! That's only one percent less than those who actually practiced!

You can teach yourself to be successful, healthy, and abundantly wealthy, by visualizing your desired outcome.

Repetition – Step two. One university study revealed that an idea which was read or heard only one time, was 66 percent forgotten within 24 hours. However, if that same idea was read or heard repeatedly for eight days, up to 90 percent of it could be retained.

So, once you've read this book all the way through, go back and read it again. This time read it with a highlighter, pencil, and note pad handy. Mark up this book. Write down the ideas you feel fit your personal business situation. This repetition will help you retain more of the information than if you read it only once.

Utilization – Step three. This is the "doing" step. It is here that neuromuscular pathways are actually developed, creating a "mind-muscle memory." And, according to the study quoted earlier, once you physically experience an action, it becomes twice as easy to recall as if you had only heard it.

Internalization – Step four. Step four is actually making the idea a part of you. This will probably involve some customization or tailoring of the idea to fit your situation or style. Never-the-less, it is vitally important for you to personalize the idea and make it "yours."

Reinforcement – Step five. Step five is maximizing the effectiveness of an idea, looking for ways to support and strengthen it. The more you can support the idea, the more you will believe it, the longer you will retain it, and the more effective it will be in helping you serve your clients' needs.

What does all this have to do with your business? Simply this: In your daily business and personal activities, as well as throughout your experience with the information presented in this book, you are going to be exposed to a number of ideas.

Some will be brand new, that is, hearing them for the first time. Some will be ideas you've heard in the past, but have forgotten. And, others will be ideas you come up with on your own as a result of something that was triggered in your mind as you read. Understanding and applying these five steps in the learning and retention process can help you retain more of what you read and experience.

Action Makes the Difference

It's important to keep an open mind as you read, hear, or otherwise experience ideas that can help you. Try not to judge them or cast them aside too quickly because they don't sound good, they're not part of your personality or make up, or because you may have heard them before.

Instead, consider these courses of actions:

- If you've heard an idea before, say to yourself, "Yes, I've heard that before, but am I using it?" If not, "Why not?"
- If you are currently using the idea, ask yourself, "How effective am I at using it? How can I 'plus,' or improve on it to make it even more effective for me and my business?"
- Next, ask yourself this question: "What will I do as a result of what I've learned?"

Remember, it's not what you know – it's what you do with what you know that counts. Ideas are powerful. And, good ideas are essential for any business. They're what keep your interest up and your business fresh, alive, and growing. Put into action, good ideas can make a huge difference in the way you do business, the results you realize, the fun you have, and the profits you make.

This book is full of good, practical, and usable ideas, which can help make that big difference for you. But it's up to you to tailor them to your own unique situation, and more importantly, to put them into action.

The Business You're In

If you don't learn another thing from our time together, remember this:

You are NOT in the (fill in the blank) business.
You are in the MARKETING business.

Read those sentences again, and again, and again. Digest them. Understand them. Internalize them. Make them an integral part of your business philosophy. Because unless and until you do, your business will be no better and no different than any of the other choices your prospects and customers can select to do business with.

Let me explain by using the insurance profession as an example, and as I do, think about how these principles might apply to your business.

It's a well-known fact that very few people (if any at all) really want to really buy an insurance policy. What they do want are the benefits, security, and peace of mind insurance provides them, their families, and/or their business. However, they don't necessarily want to spend their money on an insurance policy. But, what do most insurance sales people sell?

They sell insurance!

No wonder their business is so difficult. It doesn't take a Harvard degree to figure it out. If you sell insurance, and know that people don't want to buy insurance, why would you continue to beat your head against the wall trying to sell it?

Consider the way most people shop for auto insurance. They call up a few insurance companies and ask for a quote. The agent, or his or her representative, asks what coverage the caller is currently carrying, and gives a quote based on those figures.

The caller then thanks the agent or staff member, and goes to the next number on their list. They keep calling until they're convinced they've found the lowest price, and whichever company comes in lowest, gets the business.

But, wait a minute. Isn't there more to buying insurance than just "low price?" Well, sure there is. You and I know it, as do most insurance agents.

Why is it, then, that almost every agent, from nearly every insurance company you call, tries to sell on price, knowing there's probably someone out there with an even lower price?

Why is it that so few agents try to differentiate themselves from their competition and change the prospect's thinking away from price and on to other, more important things?

Price is important; don't get me wrong. It's very important; it carries a lot of weight in a prospect's buying decision. But it's only one of many factors a person needs to consider when making their buying decision.

In actuality, there's very little difference in insurance policies issued by any number of insurance companies in the same geographical area.

Likewise, there's usually very little difference in the products or services you sell versus the same types of products or services sold by your competitors.

General overhead costs, utilities, phones, supplies, wages, and product costs, are also similar for most companies selling like products and services.

So, if all those factors, the similarity of products and services, overhead costs and product costs, are pretty much the same, the prices charged by each individual business must, out of necessity, be pretty close as well.

It's true, that one company may, for example, obtain a lower purchase price on their products, and as a result, be able to offer a more attractive sales price for a certain period of time, but eventually, things change and the playing field becomes pretty level once again.

There are other factors not to be overlooked, such as investment income and tax write-offs, or other advantages which can play a role in the prices businesses charge for the things they sell.

But overall, all things considered, the prices charged for the goods and services from one company to another similar company, are going to be fairly close over the long haul.

The point is, no matter what business you're in, you will never maintain a long-term, competitive advantage because of the products you offer, or the prices you charge.

As soon as you develop a new product or offer a new service, it's just a matter of time before your competition latches on to it and offers the exact same thing, or maybe enhances it and offers it for a lower price. And as soon as you lower your prices, your competition can do the same thing.

The marketplace you operate in is so fiercely competitive, so cutthroat, so unforgiving, that you absolutely must do something to differentiate yourself from your competition.

If you don't, you'll be relegated to just another "me-too" business, just like all your competitors.

Now, would you like to know the good news?

Of course you would.

That's how your competitors operate: in a "me-too!" mode.

Just look around. They're all the same. Their businesses all look the same. Their products are all the same. They walk and talk the same. Their advertising looks the same, and says the same things as the next guy's. And, because they all operate that way and don't know how to change, you have a tremendous opportunity, a significant competitive advantage.

You see, if they keep on doing what they've always done, they'll keep on getting what they've always gotten.

But you, if you want to get something different,

you've got to be willing to make some changes. And that's what this program is all about. Making changes, changes that will produce real and measurable results in your business.

But, what you'll learn here isn't enough. These ideas and strategies alone, won't work. You've got to take action on them if you expect anything different than what you're currently getting.

So, make the action commitment now, and let's get started!

"Brain cells create ideas.
Stress kills brain cells.
Stress is not a good idea."

— Richard Saunders,
aka Poor Richard

1

Achieving Outstanding Business Success

Personal Traits of Exceptional Performers

Many years ago, an acquaintance of mine had the opportunity to have dinner with his friend, Earl Nightingale, the famous radio personality and producer of self-improvement cassette programs.

Earl made his life's work studying successful people and how they achieved their successes. My friend had long admired Earl for his ideas and philosophy.

He asked Earl what advice he would give his young son, if he had one. What, based on his vast experience and knowledge, would be the one thing that would help his son ensure success in business as well as in his personal life?

Earl told him, "You know, I have often thought

about that very question. And after all the years and all the study, I've come to the conclusion that your success in life, or in business for that matter, can be boiled down to one thing. That is, your rewards will always be in direct proportion to the amount of service you render.

"You only have to look around," he continued. "The people who serve others prosper. The people who don't serve others don't prosper. And, you can tell just how successful a person is by the amount of service they render to others.

"The problem," he went on, "is that unsuccessful people either haven't learned that great secret, or they don't apply it.

"The successful people are the ones who develop the habits of doing the things that unsuccessful people don't do for one reason or another."

Sage advice, indeed.

What Failures Don't Like to Do

Earl's comments were like a lightning bolt hitting my friend that night, as he realized how true they were. The more you serve your customers, and help them satisfy their needs, the more you will prosper.

As a business owner, business manager, professional, or entrepreneur, serving your customers' needs effectively, means you must do the things unsuccessful business owners, managers, professionals, and other entrepreneurs don't do. The things those unsuccessful people don't do, by the way, are the things most of us don't like to do either!

There is no doubt it is difficult to work long hours, or on weekends, when your family is waiting for you at home, and you only have a couple of "shoppers" stop by, or be stood up for an appointment someone made with you.

It's tough to make telephone calls, only to encounter people who don't really want to talk with you.

It's discouraging to set goals, schedule interviews, explain the technical aspects and benefits of the products and services you provide, overcome customers' objections and misconceptions, and go out of your way to give exceptional service, only to have your customer go elsewhere because they found the same product or service for a few dollars less.

Not only may it have happened to you, but you may have done the same thing! Perhaps you went to a brick and mortar retail store and quizzed the salesperson on the distinctions between certain models of something, and then you went on-line and made the purchase there so you could save a few bucks.

Enough of these experiences can be discouraging for anyone. And, after a while, some people just quit trying. They find it easier to adjust their standard of living downward to match their income than to adjust their income upward to create their desired standard of living.

They are no longer in control. Inflation dictates the price of things they buy, and competition and luck determine how much they have to spend. Fortunately for them, many of their competitors are in the same situation.

Outstanding success is unusual and dependent upon many different factors. For some people, it just happens. They're in the right place at the right time; they do nothing special; everything just falls into place for them. Others put in long hours and a lot of work, only to find moderate success.

A clear understanding of success principles, a well-developed and executed plan, and certain personal traits and characteristics, can help move you toward your goals more quickly.

I learned a lot from Zig Ziglar. I so clearly remember meeting him in the late '70s, when he said, "You can get everything in life you want if you will just help enough other people get what they want." This is a great core belief by which to live one's life.

Here are some other personal qualities to consider:

Eight Personal Qualities for Success

1. Know What You Want

Know yourself and exactly what you want and expect out of your business. So many people enter into business and spend years in that business environment without having any idea of what they want, or what is possible to get out of their business. It's the same in virtually every business.

In fact, most business owners are working so hard in their businesses, they don't have time to work on them. As a result, they've become slaves to their business. They've got things backwards.

They're working for their business rather than their business working for them.

Some business owners make the mistake of trying to "fit in," or be just like their competition. They watch what others are doing and spend their time and resources matching what they consider to be the factors of success; often price and availability. Smart business owners realize that when you watch the competition, you are building their business, not your own. Don't make the mistake of trying to "join the club," and hope the momentum of the industry will carry you along the path of success.

Take the time to carefully analyze where you've come from, where you are now, and what you want to accomplish in your business, your job, or your career. Then, begin to set some meaningful goals to help you accomplish your objectives. You see, if you don't know where you want to go, you'll have no idea when get there, because there is no there!

Meaningful goals are an essential requirement for success in business. With goals, you have a target to aim for, a purpose for being, and a direction to travel. Without goals, it's easy to wander aimlessly, getting sidetracked with any little thing that comes along.

I call this the "shiny object syndrome."

Something new and different comes along, almost anything, actually, comes along, and you get distracted and lose sight of your original goal.

When you set your goals, think of the word "SMART." You should have SMART goals. That is, your goals should be:

    — Specific

    — Measurable

    — Attainable

    — Realistic

    — Time-bound

It is essential your goals be Specific, so you will know exactly what you're aiming for. Your goal should be clearly defined and identified, so you not only know what you are working toward, you'll also know when you achieve it.

If you don't know where "there" is, not only won't you know when you get "there," you won't know what to do there if you get "there!"

I suspect you wouldn't want to get on a commercial airliner, hear that inevitable click on the PA system, and hear the pilot ask the navigator, "Wendy, where are we going today?"

You want to know she knows where they, and therefore you, are headed.

You are on that flight to reach a specific destination, or goal. You are the navigator of your life. Go navigate!

Just to say you want to sell more products, merchandise, or services, or reduce the number of contacts to close a sale, isn't enough. You need to clearly specify your goal. Is it 12 more sales per month? An extra $100,000 in monthly sales? How about a definitive number of certain types of products or services? How much, specifically?

Whatever your goal, there should be no doubt about what you wish to accomplish.

Your goals should be Measurable. That is, there should be a system, or method of determining how you are progressing in your effort for attainment. By clearly defining your goals, as discussed in the previous step, you will be better able to measure them. It's important for you to be able to see your current status, as well as progression toward your goals.

We've all seen those giant "thermometers," often displayed by charitable organizations raising money for a cause. They show the goal as well as the amount of funds raised. Clearly visible – it is so easy to see the goal and the status, or how far along they are. What are you using to measure and chart your goals and progress toward achieving them?

You probably remember the remarkable telethons Jerry Lewis used to host for Muscular Dystrophy. How often did they show you the goal, and how much had been raised?

Measurable is so important.

Heck, even your GPS shows you how much further it is to your destination!

Next, your goals should be Attainable. If your goal is too high, or too far out there, if there's no hope of you really achieving it, it won't take long for you to become discouraged. You may lose your focus and the drive necessary to pursue your goal, or you may abandon it altogether.

Your goal should be something you can reach with just a little extra effort.

An insurance agency owner I'm acquainted with had a large fire and casualty agency. To promote the sale of life insurance to his existing customers, the agency owner introduced a contest for his agents. The agent who sold the most life insurance would win a trip to Hawaii.

One of the agents who worked for the agency,

who had never sold much life insurance, decided he wanted to win the trip. The qualifications to earn the trip were tough, and were based entirely on the sale of life insurance policies.

Very few agents in this agency ever earned these types of trips by working the entire year for them; this particular agent put his mind to it. He qualified in only four months.

Considering the agent's past performance with regard to life insurance production, it was questionable whether he could achieve his new goal. However, he found a motivation within himself that changed the odds to his favor, and he was able to accomplish, in four months, what most agents weren't able to do in an entire year. It was an attainable goal for him, and he was able to put the effort in to reach it.

In your business operation, as well as in your life, you need to make sure your goals are not only attainable, but Realistic. If your goal isn't realistic, that is, if it's not something within your realm of achievement, it's just a matter of time before you'll become frustrated and give up. If you don't have the drive, and are unsuccessful, this may have a negative effect on you, as you begin to think of yourself as a failure, or as not being good at setting goals.

Then, because of your negative image of yourself relative to setting goals, you may give up setting goals. It's a self-perpetuating mechanism.

The key to being good at setting and achieving goals is to be realistic in your expectations. Set attainable and realistic goals which can be reached with reasonable effort. That is, unless you are like the agent I just wrote about, and you can find that motivation on such a deep level, you know you can only succeed. Failure is not an option. If your current production is $100,000 a year, and you set a goal of $1M a year, while that may feel good, is it achievable? Ya gotta be realistic.

When a goal is realistic, you can achieve it successfully. That success builds your internal success image, and enhances your self-confidence. Then, the next time, set a little higher goal. Not much higher, just a little higher. Again, one that you know you can achieve. And, that adds to, and builds your confidence, even more.

Many, many years ago, I used to teach at the marathon clinic in San Diego, California. It was not unusual for people who had never run more than a 10K to state their intention to run a marathon. Well, if all they're running now are 10K's, the potential for them to complete a marathon is close to zero. However, when they made the commitment to do the training, do the longer runs, put in the time, energy, and effort, the probability of completing a marathon increased and often became a reality.

Ya gotta set attainable goals, and do the work to achieve your desired outcome.

The next step is to make your goals Time Bound. That is, you must set a time limit for their attainment.

"A goal is a dream with a deadline."

— Napoleon Hill

This helps you keep on target, not be distracted, and encourages you to complete something you've started. Not only will this help you realize success at a designated time, but you will enhance your self-image by accomplishing your goal.

If, for instance, your goal is to sell a certain number of a certain type of product or service, or a predetermined dollar amount of sales this year, break that number down into months, weeks, and even days, if necessary.

A large goal becomes much more manageable in small pieces. The key is to break your goals into bite-size pieces, and place a time deadline on them for their accomplishment. Chunk it down to manageable pieces, or sizes.

2. The Ability to Focus

The second success quality is the ability to focus. Many people hesitate to go into business because they think they lack the talent and abilities necessary to succeed. They look at others who are successful and think they must have unique talents or capabilities. But after getting to know that person, they find them to really be quite average.

The main difference is, the successful person has developed the ability to focus, and not be distracted by all those shiny objects. A person of average intelligence, who is focused on a clearly identified and specific goal, will consistently outperform the brightest people who are not focused on anything specific.

Imagine trying to hit a target when your focus is all over the place. Texting while driving is an excellent example of not being focused. Is it any wonder why so many accidents occur when someone is texting? Just like texting while driving, if your focus is not on your primary goal, the potential for disaster is enormous.

The great quarterback has an amazing ability to focus. He sees the field, may even be aware of the defensive linesman about to tackle him, and still keeps his eyes on the receiver. How often (football fan or not) are we astonished at the quarterback's ability to thread that needle and hit the receiver in the midst of the defense crowding him?

3. Determine the Price You'll Pay

You must determine the price you'll have to pay to be successful. There is a price for everything in life, and it must be paid before you can realize the rewards. In many instances, it takes sacrifice.

A few years ago, in an effort to exercise and help relieve stress, an acquaintance of mine bought himself and his wife matching bicycles. They had fun for a while, until a group of experienced riders flew by him one day on their fast, shiny, obviously high-priced racing bikes.

Always a competitive person, he decided he would catch up to them and ride with them. However, try as he might, it was to no avail. Nothing he did would allow him to catch up to them. That ate on him for about a week, and it wasn't long before he found himself back in the bike shop getting the specifications and prices of one of those "fast, shiny, obviously high priced" bikes.

Two-and-a-half thousand dollars later, he was back on the road just waiting for those riders to catch him so he could ride with them. He was completely decked out in cycling shorts and jersey, special shoes, helmet, and his new 16 -speed racer.

Then, one day it happened. The group of riders came up on him from behind; he was determined to keep up with them. A quarter-of-a-mile later, despite his best effort, he was unable to catch up to them. The riders were gone, never to be seen again. That really irritated him.

So he bought several books, obtained training videos, and sought the help of a friend who was a pretty good rider. He worked hard, trying to develop his cycling abilities. He rode every morning, while his family was still asleep.

He encountered motorists who didn't like cyclists. Some even went so far as to run him off the road.

He'd ridden in the rain and cold weather, and

he'd ridden in 120-degree heat. He worked hard, and eventually hired a cycling coach to help him develop his skills.

Then he entered a local race; much to his surprise, he won! This encouraged him, so he entered another race. Then another. And another. And he kept winning.

With the new skills and confidence he was developing, he entered the state and national championships, placing very high in both. The riders who used to pass him were now coming to him for help and advice. They wondered how he could consistently beat them when he hadn't been riding for nearly as long as they had.

What they didn't understand was that it wasn't how long he had been training; it was what he put into his training.

It wasn't what he did during the race that counted as much as it was what he did during the long, lonely, solitary hours of training.

It was the sacrifices he made that made the difference between being a social rider or the champion he eventually became.

The same concept of sacrifice applies to operating a successful business.

If you want to reap the great and abundant

rewards your business can provide you, you're going to have to do some not-so-glamorous things at some not-so-convenient times.

You're going to have to do what Earl Night-ingale said: ". . . you'll have to do the things that unsuccessful business owners don't want to do."

The thousands of hours I invested in myself as a student when I was pursuing my doctorate of chiropractic, the thousands of hours the pilot, the physician, any professional, invests, is the price we pay to achieve specific goals.

The time you are taking to read this book, the programs, seminars, and workshops you may invest in to improve yourself, so you can be of a higher level of service to your clients, customers, and patients, are all part of that price.

For many successful people (and the fact that you are reading this book places you firmly in that category), it is about constant and never-ending improvement.

This may mean, depending on the nature of the business you have or operate, you'll have to leave the comfort of your store, shop, or office to visit with people about their needs, in their homes or businesses, at inconvenient times. Or, you may have to be away from home for some time to participate in seminars, workshops, or other training programs.

If you have a family, this may prove to be a hardship on you, but if you are just starting out in business, or want to increase your existing business or achieve some new goals, you may have to make that investment in yourself.

If you are not willing to make the necessary sacrifices, you cannot expect to be as successful in business as someone who is.

4. Self-responsibility

You are totally responsible for the success of your business and your life. There are no excuses.

There may be setbacks, economic downturns, or problems that affect your business. Your suppliers or vendors may discontinue making or providing your favorite products or services, change the way they do business with you, or perhaps merge with another company.

Economies change, corporate policies change, prospects don't buy from you, and the weather is too hot or too cold.

While those things definitely have an impact on you and the way you do business and the sales you make, it is important to realize there are those things beyond your control, and it's up to you, and you alone, to accept responsibility for the success of your business.

No matter how bad you might have it, no matter what difficulties or challenges you encounter, let me assure you: there are many people who have had difficulties and challenges far greater than any you are ever likely to experience, and somehow, they manage to pull through. You can do the same.

Here's a little credo that can help you. It contains just ten, two letter words:

"If it is to be, it is up to me."

That simple one line sentence says it all. It places the responsibility exactly where it should be: directly on your shoulders.

There is nothing to be gained by playing victim, especially to the things over which you have no control. It just is. When we live in the past, and place blame, we are refusing to be in the present, and take responsibility for what is happening now.

A very dear friend, and colleague of mine, Berny Dohrmann, Founder and Chairman of the world's oldest and largest business growth conference (CEO Space), has an expression, which I love, for when someone is living in the past: "It's not happening now."

How elegant, how simple.

There is a classic story about the acclaimed violinist, Jascha Heifez, when a stranger stopped him. "Pardon me," he was asked, "can you tell me how to get to Carnegie Hall?"

"Yes," answered the maestro breathlessly. "Practice, practice, practice!"

(True story or not, the point is made.)

Take the responsibility.

5. Be Committed

Make a total commitment to your success. Once you've made the decision to be in business, be in that business.

Get into it with both feet. Don't let anything hold you back.

Even more than getting in the business, make certain the business gets in you.

Make a commitment that you are going to succeed, no matter what.

Working two jobs, or projects, at one time can be crazy-making. You can't do either of them justice, and you'll likely end up frustrated and broke, and never know whether or not you could have been had you focused on just one project.

And, there are myriad articles supporting the idea of working on a single project as well as how to work on more than one. Only you know if you can be totally effective. Or, do you?

Current research supports the premise that multitasking impairs your overall production. Oh, I know you'll probably still go out and multi-task and handle multiple projects, so this is just for your consideration.

6. The Extra Mile

The sixth personal quality necessary to achieve outstanding success in business is the willingness to go the extra mile.

It's the "Under promise, over deliver" concept, and can be summed up in the following statement:

If you are always willing to
do more than what you get paid for,
the day will come when you will
be paid for more than what you actually do.

In his book, *Influence: The Psychology of Persuasion*, Robert Cialdini discusses what he calls the Law of Reciprocity. Basically, it says that when you do something for someone else, there's an unstated obligation for them to want to do something for you in return.

So, when you go the extra mile for your customers or clients, you've just set the stage for that law to take effect. But it's only on that "extra mile" that this works. When you give what might be considered "normal" service, or "adequate" service, or even "good" service, you haven't earned the right to expect that "law" to work for you.

In fact, even performing excellent service often isn't enough to gain you an advantage. We've all come to expect that from any number of businesses.

You've really got to do something special to gain an advantage in today's highly competitive marketplace. Then, and only then, can you expect to create that nearly compelling desire in your customer to want to reciprocate. This simple truth says it all:

"There's no traffic jam on the extra mile."

– Zig Ziglar

Taking it all a step further, what really works is to overpromise, then, over deliver on that!

In today's culture, you must deliver outstanding service.

I had the privilege of co-hosting a popular radio program in Taos. One morning our topic was service. Nancy, my co-host, owns an Adobe home, which she rents to tourists. When they are departing, she always asks them what could have been better, what would have made their stay more enjoyable?

She told me the couple who just left told her they sure would have liked an iron and an ironing board. (Nancy and I laughed; the last thing we would want to do while on vacation is iron!) Nevertheless, Nancy told them the next time they came back, not only with there be an iron and ironing board, but the third night of their stay would be for free.

The extra mile? Perhaps a mile-and-a-half!

And, brilliant. Imagine what they'll be telling their friends about their outstanding experience. Of course, the embedded invitation to come back and get a third night for free was brilliant–repeat business is always a good thing.

7. Control Your Time

The seventh quality is mastery of your time. Time is an expendable commodity. Every one of us has the same 24 hours every day. When those hours are gone, they cannot be replaced. They are gone forever, never to be recaptured.

You must treat your time as precious, and guard it wisely and selfishly. Don't let anyone disrupt you or take you away from the focus you have on your goals.

People who don't have goals are used by people who do. If you let others draw you away from your goals, you are simply saying their goals are more important than your own.

If you are serious about business success, really serious, this is one of the most important and critical areas: to defend your goals, and not surrender to another's.

Remember:

> *"Those who say it can't be done are usually interrupted by others doing it."*

> — James Baldwin

8. Persistence and Determination

Number eight is the necessity to develop persistence and determination. From time to time, you will encounter setbacks, or reach plateaus where it seems like nothing is going right.

Your competitors lower their prices, run massive advertising campaigns and unheard of promotions. The next thing you know, your customers and clients begin doing business with them.

Business is leaving through the back door faster than it's coming in the front door.

Your volume is beginning to drop, and you become concerned.

You seem to be spending more time in a defensive posture, catch-up mode, than in servicing your existing customers; and you're losing.

This is not the time to give up. This is the time to dig in and begin to play offensively.

This is the time to be determined not to lose your good customers, the ones you worked so hard to get. Your strategy should be to keep in touch with them and continue providing outstanding service and information they can use. Apply the principles you are learning in this book. Ask them who they know who may become a viable client of yours. If you ask, you may get a referral. If you do not ask, that opportunity is gone.

"If you don't ask, you don't get."

– Mahatma Ghandi

If you are spending more time in a defensive posture than servicing your existing clients, you're losing.

Have you established a referral program in your business? If not, you should. Referral business is your lifeline, and if it isn't, it is your job to establish that aspect of your business, because that will feed your business.

Do not make the mistake of assumption. You may have built a broad network of professional contacts and done the work to provide them excellent service. You may believe that each of these individuals will automatically refer business to you. You assume they understand the reason you've been so helpful. You could not be more wrong. People, even business people, are so highly focused on their own goals, they rarely think about the goals of others; unless your goal and theirs are linked. Make a point of developing the kind of connection where people really know about you and make it abundantly clear you are willing to help them without personal profit, and you expect they will do the same. The common goal is success.

Look at what services or products you provide, and talk to others in complementary businesses where you can feed each other resources and referrals.

I do public speaking. I am constantly searching for people with whom we can perhaps speak on the same stages, or market to each other's followers. Search out referral partners, people with whom you can joint venture, and you'll have another source of clients.

Know that every business is cyclical. Eventually, things in the environment will change. The one thing that should never change is your outstanding service and creativity.

While you can't be competitive on price all the time, you can be competitive on the service you provide, and the empathy you have for your customers and their problems.

We'll talk more about how to do that in a later chapter, but for now, just resolve in advance, that no matter what, you'll never give up.

Six Personal Skills

In addition to those eight personal qualities, there are six additional skills to develop that can help you achieve even greater success:

1. Effective Communication

Your ability to communicate effectively with

others is essential. You must be able to relate with other people on their level, so they understand you and what you are communicating to them.

If nothing else, remember it is your responsibility to communicate so the other person has clarity of the meaning of what you say; not the intent, but the actual meaning.

There are several levels of communication:

- You say something, and trust the other person gets it! (Good luck with that.)
- You say something and ask the other person to repeat it back to you. (Increases the probability for them to "get it.")
- Put it in writing and ask them to acknowledge it.
- Put it in writing and ask them to sign it. That's called a contract, and we all well know, even those can be in dispute.

Remember, everyone is different. Each person has their own unique communication and behavior styles; you need to be versatile enough to relate to every person according to their individual style. Be mindful to speak a language they are familiar with and can relate to; don't use "buzz words," or industry jargon.

Avoid using technical terms (unless is it appropriate), or "insider" buzz words, or private jokes. If someone does not understand even a single word, their listening is gone. They're trying to figure out what "that" word means, and everything you say for the next several moments to minutes is never heard by them.

In our workshops, we stress this by having you do exercises that anchor the importance of communicating with absolute clarity.

2. Stay on Target and Course Correct

This is the ability for you to quickly make midstream corrections. Each one of us is human, and subject to the frailties that accompany this mortal life. From time to time, we all make mistakes or errors in judgment.

The first time you make a mistake or commit an error, it is not a problem. It's when you keep making the same mistakes over and over again, without learning from them, or if you fail to quickly recover and make the necessary corrections to avoid total calamity, that you run into problems.

"The successful man will profit from his mistakes and try again in a different way."

– Dale Carnegie

I am a firm believer in learning from mistakes. I'm also a firm believer that it's best to learn from some else's mistakes!

When a rocket ship is launched to the moon, it is on course approximately seven percent of the time. The rest of the time, it is all about course correction. That means 97 percent of time it's off course! When you keep your focus, knowing where your target is, with constant course correction, you dramatically improve the potential for you to achieve it.

3. Develop Foresight

Develop the ability to spot and analyze trends. To be able to look at the past as well as what is happening today, and predict, to the best of your ability, what might happen in the future, can have a significant impact on your business success. Another word for this skill is "foresight."

In a recent interview, the president of a very large meat company told how just a few years ago, their largest selling items were canned hams. However, today, with more women working, and less time to spend in the kitchen, and more and more people having changed to healthier diets, they sell very few canned hams.

Today their mainstay is pre-cooked dinners.

Without foresight, or the ability to look ahead and predict, with reasonable accuracy, to what may happen in the near future, a company could lose its competitive position and find itself in serious trouble.

As a business owner, you should give serious thought to keeping aware of industry changes, new laws, tax laws, buying trends, and other factors that could affect you and your customers. Take whatever steps are necessary to prepare yourself to address those changes, as well as posture yourself in the minds of your customers as the expert they've come to know and depend on.

As I prepare this revision of this book, Macy's, once the major anchor store in countless shopping malls, just announced the closing of about 100 stores, with the loss of over 10,000 jobs. They did not foresee the impact of Amazon.

Borders, once a driving force in book stores, also fell to the power of Amazon. That is, they did not see what was happening to the market.

In certain industries, it is wise to keep your clients up to date regarding the current, as well as emerging changes. If you are in the financial industry, or perhaps the health care industry, or real estate, and you see where the markets are heading (that is your job, isn't it?), it is indeed your responsibility to include that information in your newsletter (you do have a newsletter, don't you?).

Remember: overpromise and over-deliver.

Let your clients know you have their best interests at heart.

This takes us right to the next subject: leadership.

4. Demonstrate Leadership

The fourth ability or skill to develop for outstanding success is that of leadership. Leadership is the ability to take charge and move others to action.

When you are working with a prospect, client, patient, or customer, and have identified and analyzed their needs, it is up to you to prepare and recommend a good, workable plan or proposal to satisfy those needs; a plan that's right for their situation and their budget.

It's not up to the client to tell you what they want. You are the professional. They have come to you for help and advice. You've got a lot more experience, knowledge, and understanding of your products and services and what they can do for them than they do. It is up to you to take charge and assume responsibility for the satisfaction and solving their problems, needs, and wants.

And, if you approach it with the right mix of professionalism, knowledge, and confidence, you'll be amazed at how many people will take your advice and follow your leadership.

When I was practicing chiropractic in San Diego, there was more than one occasion when I told a practice member that the success of their care depended upon which one of us was the doctor. Occasionally a patient wanted to direct their care, not only suggesting, but telling me what they needed. Now, I'm a huge advocate of following you inner guidance, however, offer it up as a suggestion, not as a demand of what must be done.

Imagine a non-pilot telling the flight crew how to fly the aircraft. There are times when we all must defer to authority and leadership.

It is your responsibility to take on the role of the leader, the one who really knows the why, and way.

Demonstrate that quality, and your clients, patients, and customers will honor and respect you, defer to you, and refer to you as the specialist, the one who can be depended upon.

5. Persuasive Selling Skills

The ability to sell well is an immensely important skill that can make or break your business. It's surprising how many people in business know so little about professional selling. As a matter of fact, most salespeople never study the art of selling! Selling is one of the most essential skills you, as a professional business person, can possess.

And, lest you think selling is a bad thing, remember everything in business revolves around sales. Nothing happens until someone sells something.

Many of your prospects and your existing clients know only enough about what your products or services can do for them to be dangerous (to you!); that is, thinking they know it all. They have talked to other people, read a few articles in some magazines, may even have seen a program or two on television, checked things out on the Internet, and think they know exactly what they need. In some cases, they may be close, but in most cases, they are not

Usually, they are far off the mark. You owe it

to your clients to be as effective a salesperson as you can be. Educate them, not just for the sake of selling, but for the purpose of providing them with the appropriate product or service for each individual, or company.

By doing that, you'll end up giving them better solutions and better value, saving them time and money, and helping them have greater peace of mind knowing they have the products or services best suited for them.

They will also feel good about their choice of a place of business, knowing they have just dealt with a professional who really cares about them.

You will be a beneficiary of that effort, too. You will feel good about yourself and the job you have just done for your client. That will cause you to be more effective and professional in your next interview or sale. Not only that, but your satisfied customer will be more inclined to tell others of their experience. Since you know you have done an outstanding job for that client, you will be able to employ the very powerful technique of getting their testimonials recorded on your phone, or a small camera you "just happen to have" in your pocket or purse. In our workshops, you learn how to elicit testimonials, and how powerful they are. You don't need our workshop to do this, however. The next time you have a very successful sale or a delighted buyer, just pull out your camera and ask their permission to record their happiness with the product and services you have provided. At the workshops, however, you'll learn how to achieve exactly the specific testimonial you desire.

Believe me, people respond to the personal experiences of people they respect. They'll respond to you, because a real professional and caring person or business is hard to find these days.

It's called Social Proof. When one person starts looking up at the sky, soon a few more do it. Soon, a whole bunch of people are looking up. Why? Well, if everyone else is doing it, there must be something to it.

When you say your business is great, that's wonderful. When your clients rave about you, well, that's called Social Proof.

6. Taking Action

The sixth ability to develop is that of taking action. All the things we've discussed in this chapter will not do you, nor anyone else (your clients, for example) any good if you don't take action and do something about them.

Remember, action is the key. As we discussed earlier, it's not what you know, and it's not what you talk about; it's what you do. True success in business, or in life, is an ongoing process. As Joel Weldon said:

*"The Road to Success is
Always Under Construction."*

Some people say knowledge is power. That's only part of the equation. Knowledge appropriately applied is power.

This chapter provided you with some vital knowledge necessary to be successful in business. You now have the knowledge. Now it's up to you to put that knowledge into action.

One of the best ways to have a successful business, of any kind, is to take the action to find a niche and fill it. If you're just "another one of those" (whatever it is), well, then, that's what you are. You're competing is a mass of sameness. Remember, people, including you, don't just buy what they need, they buy what they want.

You want to stand out from the crowd, right? So ask yourself, what is your unique selling proposition? What really makes you different? Find it, expand upon it, capitalize it, and grow your business.

Southwest Airlines and Virgin Airlines are both terrific examples of businesses that excel in standing out from the crowd.

Southwest (at least at the time of this writing) is the only airline to be constantly in the blue. What do they offer (beside peanuts and pretzels!) that is so different from any other airline? When was the last time you were entertained by the flight attendants reminding you how to buckle your seat belt? And, you are right, that's not enough of a reason to fly an airline, but it does speak to the attitude of the company. Of course, not charging for checking luggage may be a good enough reason to fly Southwest. And no, I do not own stock in Southwest.

Of course, if you like to know where your seat is, if you want to fly business or first class, Southwest is not for you.

The point is they fill a niche very nicely.

And as of this writing, I know Virgin Airlines has a remarkable video demonstrating the inevitable seat belt talk; their video is so outstanding it's been plastered all over Facebook. Virgin Airlines too, has found a niche and fills it: outstanding quality and service.

What's your niche? What is your unique selling proposition? How can you stand out from the crowd instead of just being another one of myriad companies or businesses offering similar products or services?

Following some of the suggestions in this book, take the action steps that will help you find answers to these questions.

Remember: Nobody "needs" a Porsche, Ferrari, Maserati, or BMW; nobody "needs" a 110-foot yacht, or a 25,000 square-foot house; people buy them because they want them.

Find out what people want and offer it to them.

*"Laughter is the shortest distance
between two people."*

— Victor Borge

2

How Do Your Clients See You?

Establish a Positive Identity

Establishing a positive identity in the mind of your customers is vitally important.

Think of the word, "professional." What image comes to your mind? Do you visualize a doctor, a dentist, a lawyer, or perhaps the CEO of a large corporation?

Did the image of the owner or manager of the business you operate cross your mind?

What criteria do you use to define a "professional?"

When you go to the hardware store and ask for assistance, guidance, or help, you're deferring to the professional there to help you.

What about other people, your clients, for example?

How do you think they define a "professional?"

The services you perform for your clients can

have a big impact on them, their family, their staff, employees, clients, and their financial futures.

The way you run your business and handle your clients' needs on a daily basis, says a lot about you, and the position you occupy in their minds.

In truth, your occupation should be viewed as being just as "professional" as any other, including doctors, dentists, lawyers, or any other type of business head.

The critical question is how professionally do you perform within the scope of your occupation?

You must think of yourself as a professional in your space, in what it is you do and what you offer.

While this program is not a sales training course, it is important for you to know that no matter what your role in business is, you're involved in sales in one form or another.

If you have staff or employees who are involved in sales, it's important for you to understand the following information.

Five Types of Salespeople

Just as different salespeople have their own

different and unique personalities, they also have different skill levels when it comes to selling and servicing their clients.

As we discuss the various types of sales-people, and classify them according to their skill level, you will undoubtably recognize some of the people you know or have encountered in the past. And as you do, take an honest look at yourself, to see where you might fit.

1. Professional Visitor

The processional visitor salesperson doesn't have any problem making appointments. In fact, they thrive on it. They enjoy visiting and talking to people, getting to know them, and may even engage in a casual discussion of their customers' problems.

Their conversation with a potential client or prospect may or may not eventually involve a discussion about how their products or services can benefit the buyers. If it does, it usually has to be instigated by the client or prospect.

A typical sales presentation will be oral, with very little (if any) use of visual materials, product brochures, or printed proposals.

2. Order Taker

The order taker doesn't mind talking to

customers, clients, or prospects, if they don't have to initiate the call. They are uncomfortable making appointments, and would rather have the customer or prospect come to them.

The telephone presents just as much a problem for these people. If the phone rings, they'll take the call and even discuss the client's needs. But it's tough for them to pick up the phone and call a client.

They operate best from a base of "low price," and have difficulty handling objections. They would rather wait until someone asks for something specific; then, they have no trouble filling the order.

3. Peddler

These are "sales-oriented" people. They have good product knowledge, but severely lack "people skills." They operate from a sort of "hit and run" approach.

This person has a good product knowledge, which they easily demonstrate to the client; however, they spend very little, if any, time establishing rapport with the client. These people are typically "product oriented," or "price-oriented." Their entire presentation is based on product, features, or price, with little regard for how the product or service will benefit the client.

The peddler is the most prevalent type of salesperson. Telemarketers who work the consumer market fit nicely into this category.

It seems like it never fails. You may have just gotten home from a day at work and are relaxing with the kids, working in the yard, or perhaps even eating dinner. The phone rings. It's for you. The person on the other end dives right into their presentation with no regard for you, the person they're calling.

For most people, this inconvenience, and the salesperson's level of incompetence, is simply aggravating. Have you ever enjoyed getting one of these annoying calls? In these types of calls, the salesperson shows no concern for your time, inconvenience, present level of product knowledge, or whether or not there's any level of need, want, or desire to know more about what they're selling.

It seems the assumption made by the caller is that what he or she is offering the prospect in terms of a product, service, or convenience, is the same or better than what the prospect currently has, and all the prospect is interested in is the price. This type of approach is an insult to the prospect or client, and is one of the biggest mistakes a salesperson can make.

4. Problem Solver

These are salespeople who enjoy getting in front of people, ferreting out problems, needs and wants, and discussing workable solutions. They have empathy for the client, can see the client's needs from the client's point of view, and enjoy helping the client solve their problems.

The problem-solving person is good at establishing rapport with the prospect or client. They enjoy identifying their needs, wants, and desires, and develop appropriate solutions, making effective presentations, and always providing a professional presentation to the client, whether it is a buyer or a seller.

However, when it comes time to ask for the order, or close the sale, they tense up, lose their confidence, or otherwise fail to close the sale. Their clients or prospects, now having their needs identified and solutions presented, go elsewhere looking for a "better buy."

This salesperson has done all the work, and an order taker for another company gets the sale and commission. After the peddler, this is the second most common type of salesperson.

5. Counselor

In the business world, it's not uncommon for companies and corporations to have a staff of lawyers, or "legal counsel," on retainer to give advice in matters pertaining to the law, taxes, investments, mergers, or other difficult or legal situations.

The sales counselor knows there is no difference between companies, corporations, or individuals, when it comes to important buying decisions. They are all to be treated the same.

To them, buying any type of product or service is a serious matter, not to be taken lightly, and can be an important tool for solving a need, satisfying a problem, or adding to their profits, convenience, or lifestyle.

They know their clients need professional and qualified representation and advice, and the counselor will do whatever it takes to provide it for them.

Like corporate legal counsel, this salesperson postures him or herself as being "on retainer," always available to give advice on matters pertaining to the products or services they sell.

They make it clear in the client's mind there is absolutely no need for them to go anywhere else for answers to the problems their products or services can solve.

The counselor knows how to establish rapport, build professional trust and credibility, identify their client's current problems, develop effective proposals, offer credible and workable solutions, and make the presentation in such a way that their clients have no question in their minds but that they must buy the concepts they present, and hence, the product or service they offer.

In addition, they have the ability to point out other problems the client might encounter, and help them solve those needs as well.

This person operates much like a professional billiards champion. Before each shot, the billiards champion carefully analyzes the position of the balls on the table to see where the next two or three shots can best be made.

Then, with precision, he makes the shot at hand, skillfully directing the cue ball to a predetermined spot so it is perfectly positioned for the next shot.

Salespeople who function at this skill level

also carefully review the client's needs, stated and unstated, and skillfully set in motion a plan to address those needs either now, or at a later, more convenient date.

Objections rarely come up because the counselor has taken the time to anticipate what objections may arise, and builds the answers to the potential objections into his or her presentation. The best way to diffuse a question or concern is to address it before the client does.

Should objections arise, the counselor either knows the solution, or is wise enough to know who to call or where to go to get the solution.

This salesperson usually secures all the business the client has, not because of price, but because the client knows the salesperson really cares about them, understands their needs, and is willing to take the time to identify those needs and offer workable and credible solutions.

How Do Your Clients See You?

How do your clients see you? I mean, when the people you deal with on a regular basis, your prospects and clients, when they view you as the person they currently do business with, or are considering doing business with, who do they see?

Are you someone they might classify as a "typical salesperson," someone who is out to sell them another product or service, or who is interested more in the sale or commission they'll earn?

Or, do your prospects and clients view you more as a counselor, someone they like and can relate to, and who is genuinely interested in them. Do you make sure they have the right product for their individual and specific needs at the best possible price? And in the event what they've purchased does not, or will not work for them, or if they're not satisfied for any reason, will you be behind them making things right?

How you answer this basic and important question is critical to your success in business. It can mean the difference between enormous success, mediocrity, or even dismal failure.

And, it's a self-feeding mechanism, as well. If you are viewed by your clients as a time waster or a product hustler, even if it is not stated, you will tend to pick up that message yourself, and act accordingly, reinforcing your client's image of you.

On the other hand, if your clients welcome you as a counselor, or an advisor, someone with their best interests in mind, someone who can help them identify and solve their problems, they will feel good about you. Consequently, you will feel good about yourself, and the role you play relative to your client. You will be and act more professionally, more confidently, and will be better able to help your client with the solving of his or her needs and problems.

As you fill the role as a problem solver, you can't help but reinforce and strengthen that positive image in your clients' minds, as well as in your mind.

What Your Customers Really Want

As a business person, it is important for you to understand that only 35 percent of the reason people buy the products or services you offer, is for the actual product or service itself.

The other 65 percent of the reason they buy is for what you can do or provide them beyond the product or service. In other words, if you are trying to sell your prospects and clients products and services, you are wasting your time. They are only 35 percent interested in products and services.

They are 65 percent interested in the benefits of having you involved.

You see, chances are good that your prospects and clients can buy the same product or service (or at least comparable ones) from any one of several of your competitors.

And with that product or service, your competitor may offer a several additional advantages as well.

They may have a lower price, better quality product, some added bonuses or extra services, a location that's more convenient, or a payment plan that is a better fit.

In today's tough, competitive market, it's difficult to compete on price or product. You may be able to command a certain advantage for a period of time because you have a lower price than your competitors, but you and I know it will be short-lived.

The truth is, you will never be able to maintain a competitive position in the marketplace, long-term, for any length of time, because of the prices you charge or the products you provide.

It'll just be a matter of time before either

one of your competitors lowers their prices or duplicates (or improves) your product, or you raise your prices because you no longer have the necessary margins to justify lower ones.

But there are things your clients can't get from any of your competitors: you, and the empathy, problem solving expertise, and the knowledge, education, and commitment to service you bring to his or her specific and unique situation.

Get involved

Products and Services, or Advice?

It is important to continually ask yourself (and be honest) the following question:

"How do my customers, the people who do business with me, my clients and prospects, see me?"

Here is an example of an easy method you can use to find out.

Take a sheet of paper and draw a line down the middle.

On the left-hand side at the top, label the column, "Products and Services."

Label the right-hand column, "Help and Advice."

Every time you are in contact with a customer

or prospect, whether on the phone or face-to-face, evaluate the overall purpose of the meeting. Place a hash mark to keep count.

Products and Service	Help and Advice
‖ ‖ ‖ ‖	‖ ‖ ‖ ‖
‖‖‖ ‖‖‖	⁄ ⁄
‖‖‖ ‖‖‖	
‖⁄ ⁄	

Did your customer or prospect look to you for the products or services you provide? Or did they seek your help, advice, or counsel, to help them make a decision that would solve a particular need or challenge they were encountering?

Once you've determined that, place a mark in the appropriate column. At the end of the month, evaluate the results of your list.

If you have more marks in the "Products and Services" column than in the "Help and Advice" column, you pretty well know what perception your clients have of you.

What you really want to do is strive to have more marks in the "Help and Advice" column. Otherwise, you will simply be perceived as a commodity, where allegiance is virtually non-existent, loyalty is a vision only you have, and your clients will change who they do business with in a heartbeat.

You know what you need to do to change that perception. You can begin to develop and implement a plan of action that focuses on improving your image in the eyes of your customers.

Test yourself again several months after you implement your changes. By comparing your evaluation sheets over the period of a year or two, or even a few months, if you're really good, you can easily see the progress you've made.

Improvement is not always difficult. Oftentimes, a person may not know where they are weak or where they need to improve. However, if you isolate those areas that need improvement, you can begin to take the necessary steps to effect positive change.

*"Live out of your imagination,
not your history."*

— Stephen Covey

3

How Much Are You Worth?

Increasing Your Value to Your Customers

You are in business for yourself. That is, you may own your own business, or you may be associated with another company or firm, either as an employee, a partner, or an independent contractor. Your working agreement or arrangement doesn't really matter.

The important thing to realize is that no matter what the arrangement or situation you presently find yourself in, you are really working for yourself. If you work by commission, for example, the sales you make are not only putting dollars in your employer's pocket, they are putting dollars into your own pocket, as well. The more you sell, the more you make.

Just consider yourself as a business that prospers or falters financially by the amount of commission dollars you generate. The point is, even though you may be working for, or associated with another company or concern, you are really working for yourself to increase the amount of money you earn for you.

Three Keys for Success

It's important to realize that your success in whatever you do in business, or in life, for that matter, will always be determined by three things:

1. The need or demand for what you do
2. Your ability to do it
3. The difficulty in replacing you

In other words, how valuable are you and the service you perform for other people?

To illustrate this, let's apply our three-step formula to the job of an elevator operator. In today's world of push-button, self-operated elevators, how much need is there for an elevator operator?

Most people are quite capable of operating an elevator by themselves; most people can push a button. It doesn't take much knowledge or training, so an operator can be replaced without much difficulty. As a result, elevator operators, if you can even find one, are not paid much.

Or, do you remember the telephone operators

of decades ago? You'd call the operator, tell her who you want to call (yes, way back then, you could just tell her [they were all women] who you wanted to call), and she would plug the cable into that person's line. Long before there was conference calling, there were "party lines," where the operator could connect several lines to connect one call.

Not much need for "her" these days, when you can directly dial virtually anyone on the planet, push the conference call button on your phone, and bridge calls all by yourself. Pretty cool.

We've come a long way, baby.

Now, contrast the elevator operator and the telephone operator of days of yore, and the money he or she commanded with that of a professional, major league baseball player. Specifically a player who is really good at batting.

What is the need for what they do? A look at attendance figures for baseball games will show that more than just a few fans are interested in watching what they do. So the need is obviously great.

How about the batter's ability to do what he does? Sports analysts say the act of hitting a ball moving toward you at over 90 miles an hour is the single most challenging movement in sports.

In the game of basketball, the target (the hoop) doesn't move. Same in golf; the cup is a static target. While the ball moves, the hole, or goal, remains stationary. In football, there are 11 teammates with a common goal of advancing the ball. But in baseball, it's the batter alone, trying to hit a small (between 2.86- and 2.94-inch diameter), 90 M.P.H. target with his bat. So it stands to reason then, the better or more often a batter can hit the ball, the more he or she will be compensated.

Now, what about the difficulty in replacing a good batter? When only the best in the world can hit the target less than a third of the time, and most of the other players are successful far less than that, it doesn't take long to realize why the best batters are among the highest income earners in the world.

What's your batting average? And, I don't mean with a baseball bat. What's your batting average with your clients, customers, and patients? You do know that those outstanding batters, quarterbacks, and other professionals, are constantly practicing and improving their game. That's one of the reasons they are at the top of their game. Remember, every true professional, from Michael Jordan, to Bill Gates, to anyone you name, has a mentor, or coach, to help them sharpen their skill sets.

You may wish to explore the workshops I offer to improve your skills in communication and negotiation.

Obtaining Superior Rewards

How about you? It's been said that you can tell how professional a person is by the size of their income at the end of the year.

You can tell exactly how valuable the service you perform is by how much people are willing to pay you for it. If you do the same job as everybody else, and do it no better than the way they do it, you can't expect to earn more money, or be considered any more valuable than those other people.

You see, the market, by nature, will pay superior rewards only for superior, or outstanding, goods and services. The market will pay average rewards for average goods and services, and it will see to it that inferior rewards are paid for inferior goods and services.

In other words, you will be rewarded in direct proportion to the value you provide your clients. It's inescapable. That's a law of nature.

Now, if the products and services you sell or provide are similar, especially in price, to everyone else's (and today most of them are), then the difference between you and other people in your position has to be in the type and amount of personal service you provide your customers and clients.

This, then, has to be the area in which you excel; it becomes your competitive edge.

Guaranteeing Business Success

So, one of the primary keys to success in business is to make certain there is a great need or demand for what you do.

One of the best ways to guarantee this is to make sure you only spend your time selling to qualified prospects. That is, people who need, want, and can pay for what you're selling or providing. There may be people who need or want what you have, but if they can't afford to pay for it, or if you can't arrange suitable payment options for them, you'll spend a seemingly endless amount of time with them and get nowhere.

On the other hand, there may be people who have the ability to pay, but have no need or want for what you are offering. In these cases, you can also waste considerable time, because surely, no sale will result from your efforts.

The second point is, you are paid in direct proportion to your ability to do what it is you do. That is, to identify and qualify prospects, sell the products and services you offer, and then service their needs as they arise.

In some businesses, the sole function of sales-people is to seek out qualified prospects and sell them the products or services offered by the business. The necessary service work for the client is provided by an office or support staff.

In other businesses, each salesperson is responsible for every aspect of their clients' needs, from the initial sale, to providing all the necessary service the client might require, including updating the product or service, client complaints, changes of address, or any other service work that may be needed.

The determining factor then, is not what your

responsibilities are, but rather, how good you are at performing those responsibilities.

Third, remember you are paid in direct proportion to the difficulty of replacing you.

When I think of this area, I think of Disneyland and Disneyworld. As attractions go, they have very little competition. As theme parks, they are unsurpassed. Their average daily attendance figures bear this out:

Disneyland – California............................35,342

Disneyworld, Epcot Center – Florida..78,082

Disneyland – Tokyo 32,877

With 146,301 guests visiting each day, and ticket prices starting at $92.00 for a one-day ticket (plus food and souvenirs), the Disney properties are light years ahead of their nearest competition. Why? Because they meet the criteria outlined in the three step formula.

Let's consider each of the steps of the formula as they apply to Disney.

First, is there a need for what they do? Well, in reality, no. No one "needs" to go to a theme park or an amusement park (although there may be times you certainly *feel* a "need" to!).

However, there certainly is a "want" to go.

Entertainment is the largest and fastest-growing business in the world, both in terms of participants, and in total dollar revenue.

Next, how about Disney's ability to do what they do? With over 60 million people visiting their parks every year, evidence suggests they are doing at least a few things, if not a whole lot of things, right.

Finally, what is the difficulty in replacing them? Nothing has come close yet; and with those 60 million people visiting the parks, the Walt Disney Company generated about $2.9 billion for its first fiscal quarter which ended January 2, 2016. Seems the odds are the people who visit the Disney properties are pretty satisfied.

The Law of Unlimited Abundance

Walt Disney was a man of extraordinary vision and foresight. He knew what it would take to be successful in his chosen area of business. He developed a formula that expressed his philosophy, and could be used in any type of business to ensure its success. He called it his "Law of Unlimited Abundance."

Walt said that it didn't matter what type of business or endeavor a person was engaged in; they could be successful and enjoy unlimited abundance if they would simply follow his formula or plan.

Walt Disney's "Law of Unlimited Abundance," stated, that to be successful, you must,

> *"Do what you do so well, that the people who*
> *see you do it, will want to see you do it again,*
> *and will bring others to see you do it."*

That's the philosophy that built the enormous successes of the Disney Empire. In their area of operation, they stand alone.

Disney's Law Can Work For You!

It can be similar in your business world, too. You see, the key is to, "do what you do," not what someone else does. You don't have to copy. You simply do your job the way only you can. That's what makes you unique, sets you apart from others, and attracts people to you.

Then, you do what you do "so well." That is, provide the type of service your clients require, want, or need, in an exceptional manner, leaving no room for mediocrity. That implies outstanding performance.

If you will do that, so, "the people who see you do it" (your clients), "will want to see you do it again (that's repeat business), "and will bring others to see you do it" (that's referral business), you too, can meet with unparalleled success.

Since so few people perform in business this way, it sets you completely apart from all the competition. Clients can't get the kind of service you offer from anyone or anywhere else. It's simply not available anywhere, at any price.

So, by default, you become unique, different, and difficult to replace. This will be reflected in your business and your income. It has to. There's no choice. It is a fundamental, eternal law of nature. You simply reap the results of what you've sown.

Walt Disney also said:

"If you can dream it, you can do it."

He did not say if you came from the right family . . .

He did not say if you have the right connections . . .

He did not say if you have enough money . . .

He simply said, "If you can dream it, you can do it."

So – go do it!

You Reap What You Sow

The question you must answer in your mind

is, "What am I going to sow, so I reap the kinds of rewards I wish to have?"

In the world of business, this is a most critical question, and one you would do well to take the time to answer. The fact is, most business people simply don't appreciate how important the answer to this question really is.

You see, many people go into business because it is something they have always wanted to do, or because they want a certain amount of freedom, or perhaps they want to be their own boss.

These are not necessarily bad reasons, but they are selfish reasons for the most part, and while they may sound good on the surface, in actuality, some of them may not be very practical.

If you go into business for selfish reasons, and fail to give the client his or her rightful due, the likelihood of your business thriving is minimal

Business, like farming, requires you to do certain things in a particular order if you are to realize an abundant harvest. Now the answer to the question, "What am I going to sow, so I will reap the kinds of rewards I want?" is simple. You only have to look at the question backwards.

First, what kinds of rewards do you want? Second, what do you have to do to get those rewards? And third, who can give you those rewards?

If you always remember, that although you may own or work for, or represent, a certain company or organization, while they may be the ones who sign your check, they are not the people who actually pay you.

Who Signs Your Paycheck?

The reality is, your client signs your paycheck. Although you must see that your company's interests are always considered, you must always keep in mind, your client is the boss.

They are the whole reason your job exists in the first place. They hire you to help them make good personal and business decisions. They trust you to help them see their problems or needs are solved or satisfied in an efficient and cost-effective manner, and they pay you well to do your job.

It is the wants, needs, and desires of your clients that should determine all your business activity. So the next logical step then, is to learn and understand just what your clients' wants, needs, and desires are. You find that out simply by interviewing and asking them. It is vitally important to listen carefully to what they say, because sometimes there may be other, hidden, or unstated, wants, or needs which may not be readily evident. Only by fully understanding these can you be of meaningful and valuable service to them.

4

Why People Buy

What Makes Your Clients Want to Buy?

You must identify the basic motives that make your clients want to buy from you.

People don't buy for the sake of owning a specific product or service. They buy because of the benefits they will receive as a result of owning that product or service.

Here is a classic example: in one year, a quarter-of-a-million quarter inch drill bits were sold, and not one person who bought one wanted a quarter-inch drill bit.

"People don't want to buy a quarter-inch drill. They want a quarter-inch hole!" – Theodore Levitt, Harvard marketing professor

People buy your products and services for the same reason, not for the product or service, but for the benefits those products or services provide. Ask the next ten prospects you come in contact with if they want to buy the product or service you're selling, and chances are you'll receive a negative answer. What they really want is the result of the product or service. You don't buy eggs for the eggs; you buy them for the omelet. OK. Maybe you buy them for the quiche, scrambled eggs, cake, or whatever; you get the idea.

There are many factors that influence the way people react that negatively impact their desire for a product or service, and all of us have our individual triggers. Regardless of individual reasons, people usually don't want to buy products, and they often resent people trying to sell them.

Remember that the next time you talk to a client.

People Buy for the benefits

If you ask the same person who previously turned you down if they want the benefits of the products or services you're selling or providing, you will most likely receive a positive answer. They may give you a hard time about the prices you are charging, but in most cases, the answer will be a "yes."

Like the quarter-inch drill bits, people are not interested in products; they are interested in the benefits the products will provide them. It makes sense then, that when you are making a presentation, you don't emphasize products.

Sell the hole, not the drill!

Instead, you should talk in about specific benefits, and how those benefits apply directly to the particular prospect in front of you.

As previously mentioned, it goes without saying: each person is different, and each person has his or her own reasons for buying or not buying. Each person will buy for his or her own reasons. Not yours or anyone else's.

If you try to sell them for any reason other than their own, you run the risk of turning them off or otherwise alienating them, which usually ends up destroying the sale you are trying to make, as well as any future sales.

Or, if you are persuasive enough, they may buy, and either return the item, product, or service, and let everyone know what a pushy salesperson you are. Not the best way to generate future business.

Trying to figure out why people make decisions can be a complicated, frustrating process, at best. But an understanding of basic buying motives can make your job much easier.

It is a well-known adage that features tell, but benefits sell. And, many people, buyers and sellers alike, often confuse features and benefits. You may describe something as a benefit, and the consumer may perceive it as a feature.

Perhaps you tell your client about the brand new Intel Xeon processor running at 3.40GHz (ask your teenager; they know what this means!). You may perceive this is a benefit (it really means the computer is fast).

A techno-geek will tell you this is a feature.

Go figure.

Who Are They Buying?

The reality is, in many situations, your client, customer, or patient, is not really buying what you're selling.

What did he say?

That's correct, they're not buying what you are selling; they're buying you.

I practiced chiropractic in San Diego for three-decades, offering leading edge health care to assist people in achieving a better quality of life; then I became a business strategist. I am also a nationally renowned speaker on communication and negotiation. What I learned over and over, is people are not buying the product or the service. People buy the person who is doing the selling or offering the product or service.

Let me explain: have you ever gone to a restaurant and asked the waitperson for a recommendation? Of course you have. If the waitperson recommends the chef's special: pasta with mushrooms, Brussels sprouts, and Parmesan (gluten free if you wish!), and it sounds remotely interesting, there is a high probability you will take their suggestion.

Or, have you asked for their opinion on a good wine?

You are again, inclined to accept their recommendation.

Why?

You believed them, not only in what they said, but in how they communicated the selection to you. If they offered a suggestion and grimaced as they told you about it, the odds are you will decline it. However, if they were passionate, enthusiastic, and congruent in the description, the probability of you accepting the suggestion increases dramatically.

So it is not the dinner special you believe in, it is the salesperson or, in this case, the waitperson.

As for my chiropractic practice, those who became practice members did so because they believed in me; that I was the person who had the expertise to help them improve the quality of their lives (as distinct from simply getting rid of their headache or back pain).

Be congruent in your language, your energy, and the message you deliver.

In my workshops, we spend a fair amount of time not just teaching, but having you being congruent. We'll talk more about this later in this book.

Motives for Buying

Behavioral psychologists tell us there are seven basic motives that move a person to action and cause them to buy. An understanding of these motives and how they apply to your prospects and clients at the time a buying decision is being made gives you a tremendous advantage.

1. Desire for Gain or Profit

Nobody likes to lose. People want something in return for their effort and hard work. The easier they can get it, the better. The success of the lottery games in various states bear testimony of people trying to find an easy way to gain and profit.

The products you sell can help your clients realize their dreams for gain or profit, too. Your clients can, and will, invest in various types of products or services you sell, not to own them, per se, but in the desire to increase their profitability and the amount and value of their assets.

2. Fear of Loss, or Need for Security

People will go to great lengths to prevent losing something. In an effort to protect their property, some people install burglar or fire alarms, smoke detectors, or night lights that automatically come on when movement is detected.

Some people carry spray cans of mace, or tear gas, while others resort to carrying guns or other weapons to protect their person.

Psychologists say the fear of loss, or the need for security, is perhaps the greatest of all seven basic motives.

If you are like most people, you will do more to prevent the loss of $1,000 than you will do to earn it.

If the products and services you sell can help protect your clients, their families, or their businesses from loss, or if you can in some way increase their security, either at the present time or sometime in the future, you owe it to them to capitalize on that fact as much and as often as possible.

3. Pride of Ownership, or Status

People want to be noticed and recognized. Little boys ride bicycles with no hands, and little girls dress up and act out dance routines and shout to their parents, "Watch me! Watch me!"

Adults do the same things, but in different ways. While they may not verbally shout out, they are still saying, "Watch me! Watch me!" just as clearly.

They do it by the kinds of cars they drive, the clothes and jewelry they wear, the houses they live in, and the material things they possess.

While people may buy because of the benefits, they enjoy it when others see the actual product. In some cases, it's just another way to say, "Watch me! Watch me!"

4. An Interest in Doing Something More Easily or More Efficiently

We all want methods of doing things more easily. You only have to look around your home to notice the abundance of time- and or money-saving conveniences we all enjoy.

What about your products or services?

Do they somehow make a person's job, or a business' way of doing things, easier or more efficiently?

And if they do, what are the direct and indirect benefits to your prospect or client?

Is this something you can capitalize on?

5. The Desire for Excitement or Pleasure

A popular bumper sticker states,

"He who dies with the most toys wins."

That message is a clear indication that people want excitement and pleasure. It seems to suggest that pleasure comes in the "having," rather than in the "getting." It's whoever has the most at the end who wins.

But in reality, "excitement" and "pleasure," for most people come in the acquiring of things.

Think back to the times you worked hard to get something, and how excited you were in the process.

But then, once you had whatever it was that you were working for, the excitement was dulled. Got it; now what?

Usually, it's not the end result that counts as much as the process of acquiring. The excite-

ment, the thrill, is in the quest, not in the attainment, nor the acquisition of "it."

Ever see a dog chase a car? Need I say more?

A more practical interpretation of the bumper
sticker might read,

"He who lives with the most toys wins!"

Of course, these statements have to do with
"things." Some people really enjoy acquiring
"things," and even keep score by how much they
accumulate.

Other people gain great pleasure or excitement knowing their family's future educational
and living needs, and their own retirement will
be taken care of.

Business owners like to know their businesses
are operating at peak efficiency and profitability,
and meeting the needs of their clients, and as a
result, will be around for a long time, providing
jobs and security for their employees and their
families, as well as providing retirement funds
for the owner when the business is sold.

Many other people are on a spiritual quest;
there is no end point. This is a life-long quest
(and beyond that if you have such a belief).
Enlightenment is not a moment in time; it is a
life-style.

Once, someone told Maharishi Mahesh Yogi, the founder of Transcendental Meditation, that he had done his mediating for the day. Maharishi told him, "You don't meditate; mediation is a way of life." It is the process, the way you do things; there is no end point.

Many people ascribe to the have-do-be model of their world.

When I have such and such, I can do certain things, then I can be certain way. When I have enough money; then I can do the things I want to do, then I can be happy.

I invite you to turn that around; change your paradigm to: be-do-have. Be the person you want to be, do the things you want to do, then you can have the things you want to have.

6. Self-improvement or an Increase in Effectiveness

Your investment of both money and time in this book (and one of my workshops, if you are so inclined) is a good example of your desire for self-improvement and increased effectiveness. People want and need to improve and to be able to do things more efficiently.

Sometimes that involves taking risks with time or money. Not all risks have to be "risky."

Calculated risks based on well thought-out plans and outcomes are the safest way to go, and can contribute greatly to the successful improvement in effectiveness and efficiency.

For a great distinction between being effective and being efficient, consider rearranging the deck chairs on the Titanic. While it may have been efficient, it certainly wasn't effective!

7. The Desire for Importance and the Need to Feel Appreciated

According to noted psychiatrist Dr. Abraham Maslow, this is one of the basic needs of all humans: acceptance and appreciation. Children want to be accepted by their parents and peers, and parents want their children to remember them when they grow up and leave home.

In his book, *The Human Side of Enterprise*, Douglas McGregor explains that workers are more motivated by "significant words," and a feeling of being needed and appreciated, than by money.

People want to make a difference, and be appreciated for it. Mothers and fathers not only have an obligation to see that their family's futures are provided for; they also want their family to understand and appreciate their efforts.

Everyone wants to be a better provider for their family, to allow their family to enjoy a better quality of life.

Business owners have an obligation to the people who buy from them, the employees who work for them, their employees' families, the suppliers, and the vendors who sell to them. Too often, each of those groups of people live with an attitude of expectancy and entitlement. That is, they expect the business owner to take care of them. How much better it would be if more appreciation would be shown to those who make our lives better?

If the products or services you provide the marketplace can help address the need people have to feel appreciated and important, you may have an open ticket to success because of the great unsatisfied need that exists.

If you understand the seven basic motives and how they apply to the business of selling your products and services, and sell to the needs and wants (both stated and unstated) of your prospects and clients, you will prosper.

If you are not prospering, it simply means you are have not uncovered your prospects' and clients' motives for buying. You are not addressing their specific needs and certainly not their wants. In most cases, you can't wait for your clients to tell you what they want. You have to be able to recognize their needs and wants.

Remember, you are ultimately responsible for the success or failure of your business. If you are doing it right or wrong, either way, the marketplace will let you know.

The Language of the Client

In which language do you communicate with your client?

I don't mean Hebrew, French, or Swahili!

We all have, what I call, a primary language through which we communicate. These languages are visual, auditory, or body-centered language, known as kinesthetic.

There are subsets of these three, and much too much information about this subject than I can cover in this book; however, a brief overview will suffice.

The visually oriented person communicates through visual images.

The auditorily centered person is more attuned to hearing rather than seeing things.

A kinesthetic person will feel things in their body.

So, to a visual, you want to paint visual pictures for their mind to see. For example, if you were selling a home you might say something like, "Can you see what it would look like coming into this gorgeous home?"

To an auditory person, you might say, "Just imagine how a really good sound system would sound in this home." Or, if they have children, "Imagine the sound of your children playing in the backyard."

For a kinesthetic person, remember this is the person who feels things in their body, you might say, "Imagine what it would feel like coming home from a day at the office, and stepping into this comfortable home."

Pay attention to the words people use, and you will soon be able to know what "language" they speak.

If you come across people who are highly visual, you may hear them say, "Can you see what I'm saying?"

Should you choose to participate in one of our workshops, we go into such great detail that you will know with certainty, how to determine which "language" someone speaks, and how to communicate most effectively with them.

You see (a clue that I am highly visual!), if you communicate using auditory language with someone who is visual or kinesthetic, it's like speaking Swahili to that person.

The Loyalty of the Client

Clients make an interesting study. It seems they always want the very most for the very least they'll have to pay. They are ruthless, selfish, demanding, and disloyal.

You know the story. Someone has done business with you for several years, and they've been great clients. You've given them the best service possible, and you think they are your clients for life. Then some little thing, possibly out of your control, goes wrong, or they see an ad, or get a call from a competitor, someone they've never met before, with a slightly lower price, and the next thing you know, they are gone, oftentimes without a single word to you.

At first you don't notice it. But one day, you realize it's been a while since you've seen or heard from that client. When you find out what happened, you feel badly, because if they would have just called you, you might have been able to make a couple of changes and save the business. But it's too late; they're gone.

This scenario is repeated time and again with businesses which sell every type of product or service. It is going to happen. To pretend it doesn't, or won't happen, is simply to be in denial.

You may even have quit doing business with someone or some company for any one of a number of reasons.

It's incredible how many business owners just write off the loss of a good client. But that's not the thing you should do. Instead, this is the time to become even more proactive and go after that "lost" client.

Call them. Let them know you notice you haven't seen them for a while. Ask them what's up. Let them know you care.

One of the best ways to minimize or cut down on the frequency of losing your good clients is to resell them on the reasons they bought from you in the first place. Regularly scheduled meetings or conversations with your clients to remind them of their motives can go a long way in helping insulate your business from the competition.

Remember, your competition has similar

products, services, and prices. Also remember your client's reasons for buying are only 35 percent based on those products, services, and prices. The other 65 percent is for what you can do for them.

Spend time with them. Review their needs, wants, and concerns. Remind them why they do business with you in the first place. Reinforce their motives, and their decisions for buying, and you will reduce your client defection rate and develop not only loyal clients, but friends, as well.

And, remember, people are much more likely to buy from friends than strangers!

Wouldn't you rather do business with a friend?

5

The Main Purpose of Your Business

Getting and Keeping Clients

Remember: profitability is priority number one. You are in business to make a profit, so you can take better financial care of yourself, your employees, and your family.

When you have an effective system that allows you to profitably get and keep quality clients who return to do business with you over and over again, and actively and enthusiastically refer you to others, your business will produce more profits than you can possibly imagine. Then everything else falls into place.

On the other hand, if you don't have enough clients buying from you or using your services regularly, it's unlikely you'll stay in business very long, and you will never have the opportunity to make a profit.

Now, let's take a minute and look closely at the

individual components of this important business skill:

Profitably Attracting Quality Clients

Clients are the lifeblood of any business. Without clients buying the products and services you have to offer, you wouldn't have a business. But clients alone aren't enough.

You want quality clients, clients who are pleasant to deal with. Clients who return to consume your products or services again and again. Clients who you can sell to, and from whom you can realize a reasonable profit.

And, you want to be able to profitably attract them. In other words, the return you realize from your investment in advertising or marketing dollars to acquire new clients should be positive. You want a positive R.O.I., or return on your investment.

Next, you want to:

Ethically Exploit Their Maximum Financial Potential

Each of your clients has certain needs and wants. The more of those needs and wants you can handle for them, the more benefits you can provide, and the more profits you'll realize.

It should be your goal to sell as many products and services to your clients as they need.

Never take advantage of them or your relationship with them. However, you should make every effort to sell them everything you can ethically justify selling them.

And, never take them for granted. They'll know, and be done with you. Just as you'll know when you are being taken for granted.

It really comes down to this, and I'll speak very frankly. If you really do provide the best products and services in the marketplace (if you don't, you'd better rethink your ethics and why you're in business), and if you really are the business which can serve your clients' needs better than anyone else (and if you're not, you either need to become that business or get out of the business), then you have a moral and ethical responsibility to make sure every one of your clients at least has the opportunity to take advantage of everything you have to offer.

And you should do everything in your power that's reasonable and ethical to give them that opportunity.

Then you want to:

Convert Clients to Raving Fans

One definition of "raving" includes "exciting admiration."

You want your patients or clients to actively and enthusiastically refer their colleagues, friends, and family members to you. You want them to rave about you.

The last thing you need is a database full of one-product, or one-service customers, who buy the minimum amount from you, complain about your prices every time they make a purchase, and give the rest of their business to the company or business that has the lowest prices or a "better deal."

There's no way you can make a profit on these types of customers. Besides, they make your life miserable and drive you crazy in the process.

What you want are clients who not only give you all (or the majority) of their business, but purchase from you repeatedly, year after year. You want clients who are so happy and so pleased with what you do for them, they actively and enthusiastically campaign for you. The story they tell about you is so compelling, the people they tell feel obligated to call you and ask for your products or services. Those are the people who make your job fun, enjoyable, and profitable.

I wrote earlier about my co-hosting a radio show. One of our advertising guests was Terry, a chimney sweep here in Taos. He became an advertiser because the week prior, my co-host (Nancy, if you recall) had Terry come out to clean her chimney. He quickly won Nancy's loyalty and trust (and a guest spot on the radio show!) because he told her she did not need her chimney cleaned!

Most of us would never know if the chimney needed to be swept. (I know, if you're reading this in Florida, you're asking yourself, "Who needs a chimney?" Well, here in Taos, it's not unusual for the temperature to get down to below zero; actually -7.6F this morning! We have fireplaces and the requisite chimneys.)

As in so many things relating to service people, we often accept what they say and go ahead with the repair or service recommendation. Do you really know if your spark plugs need to be cleaned, transmission fluid replaced, or the divariable febelhertzer tuned up? (Yes, I made up the last one.)

Generally, we accept the technician's recommendation.

Nancy had no way of knowing whether or not her chimney needed cleaning, and Terry could have gone right ahead and "cleaned" it and accepted her payment. Because he chose to tell her the truth, Terry not only earned her trust, she became a raving fan.

But wait, there's more.

After checking and cleaning the fireplace area, she said he left the area cleaner than it was before he came.

Nancy has become a raving fan of Terry's chimney sweep service because of his integrity and the quality of his service. And, as I said, she converted him into an advertiser for the radio program. Everybody wins.

There is at least one more thing you want to do with your clients…

Keep Your Clients for Life

Reliable studies demonstrate that the more needs and wants a business handles for a client, the longer they can expect that client to do business with them.

In the insurance business for instance, an agent

increases his chances of keeping an insured for three years or more by the following percentages:

- 45% if the agent insures only the auto policies
- 50% if both the auto and homeowners policies are insured
- 60% with auto, homeowners, and life policies, and
- 97% with auto, homeowners, life, and health policies!

While these figures are illustrative of the insurance business, the same principle is true of most other businesses. Banks, for instance, have studies that show the difference in client retention with customers who only have a checking account, versus clients with multiple checking accounts, a savings account, an IRA, safety deposit box, their car financed through the bank, and a number of other services.

The idea is that by serving all the needs your prospects or clients have with the products and services you provide or have access to, you lock yourself in and lock the competition out.

Obviously, the longer you retain your client, the more revenue you earn from them, the more opportunity you have to sell them additional products and services, and the more referrals you will receive from them. It all adds up to increased profits for you.

Retention of your clients, those you've spent so much time, effort, and money attracting and convincing to do business with you, is vitally important.

More than one study suggests it costs six-times more to get a prospect to buy from you than it does to get an existing client to purchase from you again, and it's sixteen-times easier to sell to an existing client than it is to sell to a new prospect.

When you add it all up, for every five percent increase in client retention, you'll generate a 30 to 45 percent increase in profitability over an 18 months.

Depending on the nature of the products and services you sell, if your repurchase rate isn't in the high 90 percentile range, you have some work to do.

A lost client is more than just a lost client and their lost revenue to you. It's much more.

In future chapters, I'll discuss how to determine the actual cost of a lost client, and what to do to prevent them from leaving.

For now, just keep this important point in mind: if you're going to be successful in business, no matter what type of products or services you sell, you've got to have an intense focus on your client. You've got to find out what they want and do everything you can to help them get it.

If you want to make a fortune rather than just a living, you can't do it for only a few people. You must do it for large numbers of people.

The success of your business depends upon how well you serve your clients: the people who buy from you!

Confused Buyers

A short time ago, I was with some friends in Santa Fe, New Mexico. During lunch, somehow we got into a conversation about people making purchases, and I said confused buyers do not buy.

After lunch we went to Best Buy. We were met by a friend of theirs who was going to buy a television. She knew what she wanted, made the decision within about ten minutes and left to return to work.

My friend wanted to buy a vacuum cleaner, so we went next to the vacuum cleaner display. The salesperson was very helpful, and explained the attributes of each of the four machines my friend was looking at. Around and around he went, querying the salesperson about each of the machines, over and over. "But does this one do this . . . and does that one . . . do that . . ." After about half-an-hour, he finally made a decision, and still wasn't certain he made the right choice. Thirty minutes to buy a vacuum cleaner?

Why?

Too many options (his wife and I were convinced any one of the machines would have done the job perfectly) led to a confused buyer. During this experience, I reminded him that a confused buyer doesn't buy, and we all laughed as he continued the adventure of examining each machine.

Confused buyers don't buy; they don't make an easy decision. They keep pondering what to do. Make it as easy as you can for your consumer so they can make a buying decision.

By the way, a few weeks after this episode, I was back in Santa Fe, having dinner with them. They told me they returned the vacuum cleaner they bought and got a different one!

There is no such thing as a confused buyer. If they're confused, they're not buying. Or at least in this situation, they're returning what they did buy.

Your Guarantee

I was talking with a dear friend about this book and some of the concepts and ideas herein. Sandra told me about a new sweater she had ordered on-line, and just received. The guarantee offered by Horny Toad (for real, that's the name of the company) is pretty impressive: "Guaranteed to impress. Wear any Horny Toad (new name is Toad&Co.) piece, and if you don't get a compliment within three wearings, send it back. Or, if you simply find something wrong with it, we'll take it back for refund or replacement. That's it. Easy huh?"

She told me the first time she wore it she got a great compliment. She was carrying the card which came with her sweater, the card with the guarantee, and laughed as she showed it to the person who offered the compliment.

How outstanding is your guarantee, or your unique selling proposition, or your product or service?

Horny Toad is so amazing (at least *I* think so),

I'm writing about it here. That is exactly what you want – people talking about you.

6

Five Primary Ways to Grow Your Business

Maximizing the Return on Your Efforts

One of the most important things for any business owner, manager, entrepreneur, or professional to realize, is there are five ways, five principle ways, to grow a business, any business.

Of course, there are many other things you can do to grow your business, but for purpose of discussion here, I'll focus on these five primary components.

The truth is that other than some administrative functions, which may not be under your direct influence or control, nearly everything you do to build or grow your business can be classified under one of five different and distinct areas, or categories, and if you learn these five simple concepts and how to apply them, believe me, your competition won't stand a chance.

The reason?

Your competition not only doesn't understand these concepts, actually, most of them have never even heard of them.

Now, here's the first one of the five ways to grow your business. Simply…

1. Get More Clients

That's it. Aw, come on, that's so basic, everyone knows that, you say.

That's true. However, let's talk about it anyway.

Build your client base. Get more prospects to buy from you and become your client.

You know how it works. When more people buy from you, you take in more gross dollars, and as a result (depending on your margins and overhead), you make more bottom-line profit.

As a spin-off benefit, the more people you add to your client base, the larger it becomes, and the larger it becomes, the more people you have to go back to for the additional sales and the referrals they're capable of giving you.

It's in this one single area where most business owners (including your competition, and probably, you, too, if you're honest), spend most of their time, effort, and money.

If you've been in business for any length of

time, you probably realize that getting a new client is not always the easiest, the most time-efficient, nor the most profitable thing you can do.

Most businesses only have one or two main methods of attracting new prospects to their businesses.

A large number of businesses are heavily into the use of telephone soliciting.

In fact, you have probably gotten more than your fair share of calls when you were just sitting down for dinner.

Chiropractors, car dealers, truck driving schools, and lawyers, take a different approach. Many of them advertise heavily on television, especially during the afternoon hours, or the graveyard time (midnight to 8 AM), to attract new clients. They've found that a large part of their intended audience, the people who are most inclined to use their services, watch television during those hours, and it's a cost-effective way to reach them.

Each business, industry, or profession, has its own methods and timing to contact those who are most likely to be interested in their products and services. What works for some businesses, may or may not work for other businesses in the same or different industries or professions.

Think about your business and your company for a minute. Chances are you, like nearly every other business owner in your industry or profession utilizes one, or perhaps two main methods of attracting new prospects.

Most likely, the method you use is the same method that nearly every other similar business uses. It's called the, "That's how things are done in our industry or profession" method.

Typically, when a person first chooses to go into business, they look around and see what everyone else is doing.

They lay out their office, shop, or place of business just like every other similar type of business they've seen.

They look at what everyone else is doing to market or promote their businesses, products, and services, and adopt those same marketing plans and methods for marketing or promoting their new business.

This copycat behavior isn't isolated to just a few businesses; nearly every business in nearly every industry or profession is guilty.

But, wait a minute. Who set up that system

you are copying in the first place? And who says it's right, or that it's the best system for you to use? The fact is, there are myriad methods of attracting new clients to your business, and your imagination is the only limiting factor.

Some of the best, most productive and cost-effective methods you can use can be adapted from what others are doing in totally unrelated businesses.

Now, this brings up a couple of questions. First, how observant are you? What are others who are in the same business as you are doing? And how effective are they?

Next, look around at what other businesses, unrelated businesses in other, unrelated fields, industries, or professions are doing. Have you seen what's working for them? Is there one business that just stands out by doing something different or unusual? Or, do they all pretty much use the same marketing methods?

The next question is, how creative are you? Can you look at what some other businesses are doing and adapt their methods, perhaps with a few minor changes appropriate to your business or industry?

In other words, if you were brand new, just

starting in business, and had no idea of what anyone before you had done to attract new clients, what would you do? How would you go about getting new clients? Would you use the same methods you use now, or would you do something completely different?

A dentist I know of specializes in working with children. He loves children. He understands that as they get older, they may need braces, and one day they'll probably get married, and then have a spouse and children who will all need dental care.

He set up his reception room with a special, "kid-height" counter, so when the children come in, they can talk directly to the receptionist, transact their business just as an adult would, and schedule their next appointment. He's even decorated his reception area with artwork and pictures some of his young patients created.

How do you think those young people feel? Well, you probably guessed it. They absolutely love it there. They tell their friends about it, too. Their parents? They're thrilled.

Imagine having your kids want to go to the dentist and be treated, not like a second-class citizen, but as an equal, transacting business (with the parent's help, of course), and having a hand in scheduling their future appointments.

What a learning and growing experience for them. Who do you think the parents use for their own dentist? That's right.

The spin-off business of catering to, and working with children, is their parents.

As the kids grow up and have families of their own, which dentist do you think they'll use, who they'll insist their spouse switches to, and they'll bring their own children to?

The relationship of friendship, trust, and caring this dentist is building with those young people will provide him an abundant pediatric and adult practice, and all the financial security he'll ever need, which will allow him to do whatever he wants, and go wherever he pleases for the rest of his life.

Talk about copying someone else's idea . . .

When you think of the drive-through, the odds are you think of McDonald's. Yes?

Well, believe it or not, they were late to the game.

The first-drive through? A Texas chain of eateries called the Pig Stand, on a highway between Dallas and Fort Worth. The year was

1921. McDonald's wasn't to come into existence for another 34 years!

Who picked up on the drive-through very early on?

In-N-Out Burger, which started in 1948.

It wasn't until the mid-'70s that McDonald's began experimenting with the drive-through.

Ya see, sometimes it does pay to copy someone else's idea.

So, what about you and your business? What are you doing? Specifically, what marketing methods are you using right now to attract new clients and build lasting relationships with them so they'll do business with you for a lifetime?

And second, how many different marketing methods do you presently and concurrently have working for you? There's a real danger in having just one or two main methods of attracting new clients.

I know someone who depended almost entirely on a telemarketing company to acquire leads for their salespeople. When a well-funded competitor opened for business and hired nearly all that business' telemarketing staff, they almost had to shut their business down. It was nearly a total disaster.

They had to do something quickly to save their business. They hired and trained a whole new telemarketing crew, and got the business up and running again.

They then looked at other marketing options and put together an effective direct-mail program, started a proactive referral-generating system, and worked out some joint ventures and host-beneficiary relationships with other, complementary, but non-competing businesses.

Now, if something happens to any one of their marketing methods, they have other strategies, other "pillars," in place that can keep the business from collapsing, and keep it running smoothly.

What about your business? How can you apply this?

Why not start by going back and revisiting the questions I asked earlier? Then see if there are some areas you need to improve in.

Make sure you're not dependent on only one or two main methods of attracting new clients.

New clients are essential to your business; there's no question about that. They're not just important, they're absolutely vital to the growth and very survival of the business.

It's critical you have multiple systems in place to ensure that your business continues running, and growing, uninterrupted, if anything unexpected happens.

This book is not intended to cover all the possible methods of getting new clients; no single book can. However, in the training materials and workshops I conduct, I go into great detail on effective ways to attract prospects by the bushel, and convert them into loyal, long-term clients.

My programs and workshops also offer myriad resources for communicating and negotiating with potential clients and patients, as well as your existing ones.

As important as getting more new clients is, there are still four more basic methods you can use to grow your business. Each of these methods is more profitable, more effective, and will give you greater potential for leverage than the first method.

Let's talk about number two:

2. Suggestive Selling – Or, "You want fries with that?"

In other words, increase the average transactional value of their purchases. Or more simply, get them to spend more money when they buy something from you.

This just happens to be the quickest and easiest way there is to increase your profits.

One of the things that continually amazes me is the number of businesses that have extensive and expensive plans in place to acquire more clients, yet they have little to no emphasis on this highly profitable, and highly leveragable way of increasing the size of the order, getting more money from each of your clients every time they buy from you.

If you think for a minute about how easy this is and how profitable it can be, you'll see why it's such a powerful concept. And, you'll also see why nearly every fast-food restaurant has embraced, and mastered this principle, and requires every person who takes orders, to understand and be proficient in the use of the "upsell" and "cross-selling" principles.

Think back about your own fast food restaurant experience. You order at the counter, or drive up to the speaker and place your order, a sandwich and a drink. And then what happens? You are asked a simple question: "Would you like fries or an apple pie with that?"

That's an example of cross-selling, which is selling an additional product beyond the initial purchase.

Or, they may suggest that you "super-size" or "giant-size" your order. That's an example of an upsell, increasing the size of the initial order.

Upselling is essentially the art of generating free money.

If you take them up on their suggestion, what they've done is just increase their profits substantially, since they made an additional sale, but had no acquisition or marketing costs.

You see, they realize a certain percentage of their clients will say, "Yes." The only reason they say, "Yes" is because a suggestion was made to them, or a question was asked. So the seller plays the numbers game knowing some will indeed, say, "Yes."

Amazon is another example of up selling. When you check out, you see what other people who made the same purchase also bought, ostensibly encouraging you to make similar purchases.

From car salespeople to insurance salespeople, and beyond, those in the know, upsell.

Need some more examples? (You may recognize how often you have been on the receiving end of some of these suggestions!)

When purchasing shoes, have you been asked if you want socks, or shoe polish, or perhaps shoe trees?

Been to a hair salon? Been asked if you want styling products?

How about when buying electronics (stereo receivers, televisions, cell phones, etc.), and being asked if you want the extended warranty. And, specifically with cell phones, the carrying case, the screen protector, and earbuds.

The result? Well, by being aware of what your clients want, but may not think to ask for on their own, and simply asking questions or making suggestions, you have the potential to generate substantial additional revenue. There is no marketing cost associated with these additional sales, so, other than the actual cost of the product, those dollars are pure profit. Here's another technique fast food restaurants frequently use. It's called "bundling," or "packaging."

This is where they combine a sandwich, a drink, and fries, and then throw in a couple of "bonus" items, like maybe a cookie and a toy.

They put it all together in one package, and give it a name like "Happy Meal."

They'll charge you less for that package than what each of those items purchased separately would have cost, but the total dollar amount you spend will be higher because you would never have purchased all the individual items. Pretty clever, wouldn't you say?

Since there were no marketing costs involved, other than the cost of the items themselves, this sale generates pure profit, and it goes straight to their bottom line.

Which other types of businesses are masterful at bundling? Your cable company and your cell phone company. It is highly unusual for someone to have basic cable, or basic cell phone service. They offer additional services, and tell you how much money you are saving by bundling the services.

Now, what does that have to do with you, and your business?

Well, you may not be in the fast-food business, but the same principles can still apply. Just ask yourself this question: "What additional products or services do I have that would be natural complements to what my clients initially buy from me?"

Well, you know the answer to that. And, if you don't, this is a good time to start thinking about it. If you have the type of business that offers more than one product to your clients, you have a tremendous opportunity to capitalize on the up-selling, cross-selling, and bundling techniques.

Some types of businesses, such as insurance companies, which may offer only one product or service, can also benefit from these strategies by packaging certain policies that cover multiple family members, adding riders, or including other complementary services that go beyond the actual policies themselves.

Do these things seem like common sense to you? They probably do. However, as I mentioned before, it's surprising how few businesses make effective use of these three simple principles.

Mike Crow founded a home inspection company and now teaches home inspectors to upsell, or bundle services by asking the home-owner if they would also like a pool inspection, a sprinkler system inspection, a termite inspection, etc. Mike coaches home inspectors on how to duplicate what he's done for his businesses: that is achieve a ten-fold increase in his revenue. He's done so well in his niche market, he now teaches other small business owners (his model applies to virtually all businesses how to increase their revenue and how to build more successful businesses). You can find more about Mike at coach-blueprint.com.

Examine your business very carefully and see where you can upsell, cross-sell, or bundle.

Think about it. In reality, you have an obligation to your clients, the people who trust you to provide them high quality products and services, and who hand over their hard-earned money to you to give them sound advice, and to make sure they get the very best value, the best use, and the most enjoyment from their original purchase.

And if you have additional items that can enhance their value, their use or their enjoyment, then your obligation is to do everything that's reasonable and ethical to see they at least have the option of taking advantage of those items.

Again, it's playing the numbers game. Some will take advantage of your offer, and some won't. At least you will have given them the opportunity, and you will have fulfilled your obligation to them.

You haven't made the decision for them. You give them a choice, and let them decide.

If you are sincere, they won't see you as being pushy. They will know you are really trying to do them a favor and trying to help them get more value, more use, and more benefit from their decision and their purchase.

They'll come back to do business with you again and again, and will refer others to you as well.

Upselling, cross-selling, and bundling, are only three of more than a dozen immediate, profit-producing methods you can use to skyrocket your business to the next level.

If you do nothing more than find a way to incorporate these three techniques in your business (which you should be able to do within the next twenty-four hours), you'll blast your profits completely through the roof.

Think about it: increasing your sales and increasing your profits without increasing your expenses! It's an exciting concept, and it can add an immediate twenty, thirty, even forty percent or more of pure profits to your bottom line!

Only offer additional products or services directly related to what the client is purchasing, and remember, the appropriate time to offer the up sell is after the client has made the commitment to buy. Consider making an upsell as a "two-fer" offer; offer the second item at a reduced price. You'll see a lot of pizza commercials for this!

3. The Value of the "It"

Remove the word "dollars" from your vocabulary.

What does that mean?

The word dollars has a huge emotional tag. To increase the dollar amount your client purchases, reduce the emotional impact of the dollar value of the sale.

So, if you're selling a conference for example, and you explain the value and then tell the prospect the investment is $7,500, there's an emotional anchor to the $7,500.

However, if you simply say the investment is "7,500," you have lessened the emotional impact.

Of course, when the check clears the bank, the amount is the same.

No matter what you are selling, whether it's

a home, car, an oil painting, etc., eliminate the word "dollars."

You will rarely hear a (sophisticated) Realtor tell you the home is available for $597,000. They will simply say, "597,000."

But wait there's more.

Although I just said to eliminate the word "dollars," there is indeed a time to use the word.

Remember our discussion of how using the word "dollars" raises the emotional value? So, when you're offering a discount (and in our workshops we talk about when and how to offer a discount), you absolutely use the word dollars.

For example, if you're selling a home, you might say something like, "This house is listed for 650,000 (notice the absence of the dollars), however the seller is motivated, and may be willing to offer a $50,000 discount. Notice the inclusion of dollars here, to increase the perceived value of the discount. "So, you can have this home of your dreams, for only 600,000."

If you're making an offer on something, absolutely include the word "dollars." Again, this increases the emotional impact, and in reality makes it sound to the seller as if you have offered a higher value. More than words games; you are changing the emotional impact.

Please understand, in a written document, you must use the dollar sign; these examples are for the spoken word.

Really?

Cornell University's Center for Hospitality Research, in 2009, found that removing the dollar sign significantly increased sales at St. Andrew's restaurant in New York.

And again, when you attend my workshop we go into more depth with this.

Now, let's move on to the third way to grow your business . . .

4. Get Your Clients to Buy From You More Often

In other words, increase the frequency of their purchases. Get them to come back; give them reasons to want to come back and to continue doing business with you. The longer your clients go between purchases from you, the more chance there is they will buy from your competition.

It's like, "Out of sight, out of mind." You need to constantly stay in front of your clients with educational information, and notices of changes in the law, or updates regarding the products or services they've purchased from, you that can affect them. And you need to tell them about new products, new lines, special incentives, and other offers that might benefit them.

The idea is two-fold: one, to "lock" your clients in, so they can't afford to do business with anyone else, and secondly, to make it so attractive to do business with you, they wouldn't even consider going anywhere else.

What you really want to do is lead your clients to the inescapable and undeniable conclusion that they would have to be completely out of their minds to even consider doing business with anyone else but you, regardless of the selection of products or services you provide, the prices you charge, your location, or the relationship they may have with the business they're currently doing business with.

You want to create, and sustain TOMA, or Top of Mind Awareness. That is, whenever they think about the type of practice, business, or service you provide, or offer, you are the only one they think of.

It's not a choice between you and someone else; there is actually no choice – it's only you. Here is a real-life example of how this works:

A restaurateur who offers his business clients who like to take their clients to lunch, a certain number of lunches for a pre-paid, discounted price.

By doing this, he "locks in" his client, gets his money up front, and makes it convenient for everyone. The client simply signs the check, which includes the tip. No money changes hands during or after the lunch, and new clients are constantly being introduced to his restaurant. As a result, many of those new clients take advantage of the same arrangement for their clients.

And, you'd better believe the client is impressed that their host has such a great relationship with the restaurant. This creates a powerful image of the host in the client's mind. Conversions go up. And, the guest of that client is more inclined to frequent his or her new-found favorite restaurant!

Here's another example: the car wash where I take my car offers a special pre-paid, discounted card that's good for a certain number of car washes. It's a great deal for me because I save money, and I can take my car to be washed, even if my son got into my wallet and took the last couple of dollars I had.

And when my card is filled, I've got a free wax job. It's a good deal for the car wash too, because they've gotten their money up front, and have locked me out of the competition.

Here's one more. The hardware store I shop in offers a "rewards" program, where for every $100 I spend in the store, I receive a coupon in the mail for $10. That is, in essence, a 10 percent discount, and certainly keeps me going back to that store instead of one of the other hardware stores. And, I'll typically spend more than $10 on the next, "free" trip.

Cid's, the organic grocery store where I shop, gives shoppers a chip, worth 10¢, for every reusable shopping bag they bring in, instead of using a new paper one. They have arranged for shoppers to be able to donate those 10 cents to 30 different local, non-profit organizations, and Cid's matches the funds! I live in Taos, New Mexico, a small town, and these donations keep clients coming to that store instead of the others. The other day I was talking with Cid Becker (of Cid's); he told me the cost of bags is 11¢ each. We'd all love to see the other grocery stores do the same thing, instead of giving shoppers 5¢ off the bill when you bring your own bag. Last year

Cid donated nearly $30,000 to local non-profits. This program keeps Cid's at top of mind awareness with clients and scores huge points for its reputation as a caring, contributing member of our community. Where would you rather shop?

Airlines offer upgrades and mileage bonuses for those who fly with them on a regular basis. Countless other businesses offer similar programs, all designed to keep their companies top of mind.

Now, let's apply this concept to you and your business. What can you think of that you could do that will endear your clients to you? To lock them in, and get them coming back more often and, even refer others to do business with you?

Do you have an educational newsletter or special informative reports you periodically send them to keep them updated?

Do you send postcards; do you have a website that keeps them informed of new items and promotions?

Do you hold special "Client Appreciation Sales" or events? Using Cid's as an example, every year they have an anniversary celebration for two days, where you can pick up their branded, reusable shopping bags, as well as win one of the countless prizes. The store is absolutely packed for two days. Don't know how much, but from seeing everyone's shopping carts so full, I'm confident the revenue from those two days is outstanding. What can you do?

Do you gather your client or patient's e-mail address so you can let them know about your special events?

How about a Frequent Buyer Club for your more loyal clients?

What about a Referral Reward System that recognizes or compensates your clients for referring their colleagues, friends, and family members?

You've got to let your clients know you value them, you appreciate them, you want them to come back, and you want to make doing business with you fun, risk-free, rewarding, and easy.

We have two hardware stores in Taos, and I wrote earlier about the one with the rewards program. A few months ago, I purchased something at the other store, and later needed to return it. They would not take the item back because I did not have the receipt. They were unwilling to bend the rules (the item had their store label on it, so there was no question as to where it was purchased). As a result, they lost my business. The other store, now has it.

Nordstrom follows an outstanding model of making the client right. It is my understanding they'll take returns on merchandise they don't even sell! Ya gotta love doing business with them.

I was a principal and an investor in Graham's Grill, a start-up restaurant here in Taos. Part of my responsibility was to write the policies and procedures manual. One of the things I included was giving the servers not only the responsibility, but the authority to ensure the client was made right. If something was not right with the meal, the server had the authority to offer a free dessert, a free drink, or even a free dinner; it was the server's responsibility to ensure the client was well taken care of.

Shortly before the grand opening, I bowed out of my relationship with Grahm's. I have been told by several people who have eaten there, that that segment of my policy manual was never implemented, and that all too often clients were actually made wrong.

In fact, I have heard that it was so bad that the owners were known to denigrate the servers in the presence of clients. Not surprisingly, they're no longer in business.

How do you feel when you're in a problematic situation, and the salesperson, server, or person you're talking with says, "I'll have to get back to you on this?" In your business empower, those with whom you work to make decisions. Everyone wins.

I recently met with some of the most successful business leaders in our town; we discussed their conclusions about what has contributed to their outstanding success. There was a consistent theme: be selective in your hiring, train your people well, pay them well, and empower them to make proper decisions.

We also had a surprising conversation about employees being employees. You are not their mother or father nor their best friend. They all said the same thing: it was a mistake when they socialized with their employees, because then the employees essentially had no respect for them. In 2008, when the economy took a serious downturn, and employees were asked to work extra hours and forgo pay raises, they quit. They were not part of the team. They hired new employees, honored and respected them and treated them well as employees. These employers have had the same teams for five years. Loyal employees, who are paid well, feel appreciated, and are acknowledged for their performance and what they do, will stay with you.

There are many leaders of businesses, both large and small, who believe in hiring cheap and replacing employees as needed. When you consider the cost of losing and replacing employees, this is really a stupid model. National estimates show that an employer will pay about 20 percent of the annual salary of an employee earning less than $75,000 a year when they have to replace that employee. There are other estimates that range as high as 213 percent. This figure includes not only the cost of the actual training, but the revenue lost from lost sales, lost clients, mistakes in production, etc. Lose a key player, an executive, for example, and the cost could be incalculable. Be wise – take better care of your employees, treat them with honor and respect, and pay them well.

I'm confident you can see the ideas are unlimited. And while the restaurant, car wash, hardware store, and grocery store examples may not apply directly to your business, I've included them to serve as a stimulus so you can begin thinking of what you might consider applying in your business that can help you develop trust and loyalty with your clients. Again: TOMA – Top of Mind Awareness.

In our coaching programs we go into great detail, and discuss very specific strategies that create an almost magnetic effect to keep your clients returning time and time again.

We lead you by the hand and help you develop personalized and effective strategies that keep them saying, "I'll be back," strategies that keep them "insulated" from, and locked out of your competition.

During these workshops you will also learn the seven words which can potentially decrease what you pay for something, and increase what you get when you sell something.

Now let's talk about the fourth method you can use to grow your business.

5. Your Community – Be a Part of it

I wrote about top of mind awareness and how important it is. Participation in your community will contribute massively to top of mind awareness, where your name, your business, and what you do with the community become so pervasive, everybody knows you.

You already know I live in Taos, a community of 5,000 people. About ten-years ago, Mary Domito moved to Taos, saw a need, and eventually established a business called Taos Lifestyle. Taos Lifestyle sells mattresses and home furnishings. Brilliant at branding, Mary took on the moniker of "Mattress Mary." Everybody in town knows Mattress Mary. If there is a function or an event, Mary is one of the largest contributors and sponsors. Her name is constantly on the air as an advertiser; she was a frequent guest on the radio program I co-hosted. She is also a significant advertiser in our weekly newspaper, a member of the Chamber of Commerce, and a member of our local entrepreneurial group, the Taos Entrepreneurial Network. Mary's business flourishes.

Wolfgang Collins, who calls himself "a declared immigrant," opened Wolfgang's Spa Works, here in Taos, some years ago. There were three other spa businesses in town when he opened. Wolfgang is a member of the Taos Chamber of Commerce, the Taos Entrepreneurial Network, and advertises consistently on the radio and in the newspaper, creating top of mind awareness. He is now the only spa business in Taos. He told me a story about when he followed his wife's suggestion, and they ceased advertising. She felt that since they were the only game in town, they could save the money they were investing in advertising. In a heartbeat, top of mind awareness was gone; the phone literally stopped ringing for three months. After that failed experiment, we hear his commercials all the time, see his advertisements in the newspaper all the time, and see him at events. He finds it amusing, and very profitable, how many people decide to purchase a spa because there are commercials and advertising for Wolfgang Spa Works.

Get it? Get into your community, contribute, not to get, just to give. The payback will astonish you.

Extend Your Clients' "Average Buying Lifetime"

That's "Client Retention."

Here's what I mean: How long, on average, do the people who buy from you, your clients, remain your clients?

In other words, how long do they continue doing business with you before they move on? Are they one-time buyers? Do they stay with you for a year, five-years, ten-years? Have you ever stopped to figure it out? This is an important step, and one that will be discussed in more detail in later pages.

Next, what are you doing in your business right now, to make sure your clients continue doing business with you? If you don't have a strategic plan, a working system in place, you are going to lose a certain percent of your current clients to the competition.

There's no question about it. Your competitors, right now, right this very moment, are making plans and taking steps to take your clients away from you.

The question for you is not, "What are you going to do about it?"

The real question is, "What are you currently doing about it?"

"What are you doing about it right now?"

What plans, what systems do you have in place to keep your clients from defecting to the competition?

Let's talk about your clients for a moment.

Are they thrilled enough with the products you offer and the services they receive from you to continue doing business with you year after year?

If you answered "yes" to that question, my next question is, "Are you sure?"

"How do you know?"

"Where did you get your information?"

"How reliable is it?"

"Can you explain in detail the system you have in place for finding out?"

Notice that I said, "Are they thrilled enough?" Not, "are they satisfied enough?" You see, there's a huge difference between being thrilled and being satisfied.

In 2012, more than 200 million Americans stopped doing business with companies with which they were "satisfied." Sixty percent of so-called "satisfied" clients switch companies or brands on a regular basis.

As a business owner, you can't afford not to thrill your clients; you have to build their trust in you and your business. The cost of losing clients is too high, and unfortunately, most business owners simply don't understand that. Let's take a look at what the potential cost could be to you if you fail to do these things.

Let's say that you make $200 in sales per year from your average client.

And, for any number of reasons, 100 clients stop doing business with you each year. They may die or move away. They may no longer have need for your products or services. They may switch companies, have a relative go into the same business, or possibly have a bad experience with someone in your company.

Or, they may just simply disagree with some policy or procedure you have. It could be a falling out with a staff member or employee, a personality conflict, miscommunication, a problem they had with one of your products, or perhaps a feeling of neglect from you or someone in your business. It really doesn't matter what the reason; they just stop doing business with you.

Those 100 clients, no longer paying you $200 this year, just cost you $20,000. But that's not all. What if those 100 clients tell five others about their real or imagined bad experience with you?

That's an additional 500 or so potential clients who won't be doing business with you this year either (or maybe ever, for that matter).

And if each of them spent an average of $200, that's $100,000 you won't be receiving from them, plus the $20,000 you lost on your existing clients who left.

That brings the total in lost revenue to $120,000 in just one year!

It's not unusual for some businesses to bring in a hundred (or more) new clients each month. That's twelve hundred-plus clients a year. And they end up only netting a 150 or 200 increase at year-end (sometimes not even that).

What happened to the other more than 1,000 clients? Where did they go? Surely, they all didn't die or move away.

Most business owners don't concern themselves with what, or whom they've lost. They just focus on their net gain. They figure that if they finish the year with more clients or more sales than they started with, they're ahead.

Now, let's suppose you gave those 100 lost clients good, compelling, life or business-enhancing reasons to continue doing business with you this year.

And let's suppose each of them told those same five people about their positive experience with you.

Well, there's $20,000 you wouldn't have lost in the first place, and another $100,000 you may potentially pick up from their referrals or by their word of mouth.

The point is, clients are important; all clients. In fact, they're critical. There's no question about it. You and I know that. A business couldn't remain in business unless it has someone to buy its products and services.

Those "someones" are people. Real people. People like you and me. If you sell your products to the business community, remember, businesses don't buy from businesses.

People in business buy from other people in business. It's people you market to. Not businesses.

Here's an interesting point: Most business owners know exactly how much they have tied up in furniture, fixtures, and equipment. They can tell you, nearly to the penny, how much each item cost, how old it is, how much it's depreciated, and what the remaining life expectancy is.

That's important information for any business to have. There's no question about it. But what's amazing is that very few business owners have any idea of the value of their most important asset: their clients.

Think about how this whole concept relates to

your business. What is it that you can do, specifically, to extend your client's buying lifetime with you? Why not take a few minutes and answer these questions?

First of all, who are your clients, those who are buying from you now?

Who are their family members?

Do you know the names and ages of their spouse or children?

Do you know their anniversaries, birthdays?

Do you know where they work?

What about their spouse or children?

What are their hobbies or interests?

Do you know why they purchased a particular type of product or service?

Do you know who their friends, neighbors, or relatives are?

Do you ask them, as Nancy did with her out-of-town guest, how you can improve their experience with you?

What about your staff or employees? Do you know how they treat or feel about your clients?

Do you have favorite clients, customers, or patients? What makes them a "favorite?" Is it how much they spend? How often they come in? Their personality?

How do you treat those people? Any differently than the others?

What would you have to do to have more people like them consume your services?

Do you have regular staff meetings and talk about how to think like a client?

What would you want if you were a prospect considering doing business with you for the first time? Or maybe an existing client considering giving repeat business to your establishment or organization?

Or, perhaps considering referring a friend, a family member, or an acquaintance?

Do you have a training system in place to teach your staff how to handle or deal with challenging clients? Short-tempered clients? Analytical clients?

Do you have a plan for moving people up the "Loyalty Ladder?" From Suspect, to Prospect, to Shopper. Then on to Customer, Client, and Advocate. And, finally, to convert them into raving fans?

When a client stops doing business with you, do you know why? Do you have a system in place to find out?

What would you have to do differently to get

your clients to buy from you for, say, five-and-a-half years, instead of just five years?

Believe me, if you take the time to go through these questions and formulate answers to them, and then incorporate that information into your business practices, you can work wonders toward extending the buying lifetime of your clients. As a result, you'll add significant profits to your bottom line.

Ah, the distinction between a customer, about whom you know nothing, and a client, about whom you know a bunch.

We've covered a lot of ground and a lot of ideas so, let's pause for a minute, and recap what we've discussed up to this point.

A summary of the five primary ways to grow a business:

1. Get more clients. As I mentioned, this is a vital step. But it's also the most difficult and the most costly.

2. Get your clients to spend more money with you; increase the average transactional value of each sale. Remember, this is the fastest and the easiest way to add immediate profit to your bottom line.

3. Eliminate the emotional impact of the word dollars.

4. Get your clients coming back to buy from you more often.

5. Extend your client's buying lifetime. Find ways to retain them, keep them as clients, and keep them coming back as long as you possibly can.

It's really pretty simple. Nearly everything you do to build and grow your business can be slotted into one of these five categories.

As I mentioned earlier, there are myriad ways to apply these concepts and build your business, but for now, if you'll work on these five primary methods, you'll absolutely run circles around your competitors.

As you take a good, close up look at these five areas, you'll see what it really boils down to is effectively marketing your business to your clients and potential clients.

In other words, the success of your business depends, largely, on how effective your marketing system is.

That means if you want your business to excel, to really excel, if you want to virtually eliminate your competition, and become the dominating force in your marketplace, you've got to begin thinking of yourself as being in the marketing business, not in the product or service selling business.

While you may be a master at your trade or craft, you must think of yourself as the person marketing your trade or craft or business.

In effect, you need to consider yourself as the head of a marketing organization that sells the products and services your business offers.

Once you begin operating effectively at that level, you'll find your job becomes much easier and much more enjoyable, and your prospects and clients will begin seeking you out and referring others to you, rather than you chasing after them. The net result will be that your marketing costs will plummet, and your profits will skyrocket!

Know Your Value

The value of your knowledge, wisdom, and experience, is what people are investing in, or paying for. There is a classic story about a woman at a crafts fair who saw a beautiful piece of macramé she thought she would like to have. She asked the vendor the price of the macramé.

He told her she could have his magnificent work of art for $197.

"One-hundred-and-ninety-seven-dollars," she exclaimed in shock, "why it's only a piece of rope!"

The artisan slowly grasped one end of the macramé and proceeded to undo his craft, knot by knot, inch by inch, until he unfurled the entire length of the rope, which he graciously handed to the woman, and said, "Madam, the rope is free."

Remember, the cost of the production is not what someone is paying you for. They are paying you for your knowledge, wisdom, and experience; your life's work.

Another of my favorite stories along this line is the story about a ship's engine that failed. The ship's owners tried one expert after another, but none of them could figure but how to fix the engine.

Then they brought in an old man who had been fixing ships since he was a youngster.

He carried a large bag of tools with him; when he arrived, he immediately went to work. He inspected the engine very carefully, top to bottom.

Two of the ship's owners were there, watching the old man, hoping he would know what to do.

After looking things over, the old man reached into his bag and pulled out a small hammer.

He gently tapped something. Instantly, the engine lurched into life.

He smiled and carefully put his hammer away. The engine was fixed! The ship's owners were ecstatic. A week later, they received a bill from the old man for ten-thousand dollars.

"What?" the owners exclaimed. "He hardly did anything!"

They wrote the old man a note requesting an itemized bill.

The man sent a bill that read:

Tapping with a hammer....................$2.00

Knowing where to tap............... $9,998.00

It's not how long it took, nor what was involved.

Remember, you are being paid for your life's experience, your life's work.

*"Only a life lived for others is
a life worthwhile."*

— Albert Einstein

7

How Much Are Your Clients Really Worth?

The Lifetime Value of Your Clients

You must know how to determine the lifetime profit value of your clients.

There's not much debate about this fact: your existing clients are your most valuable assets. The question, is how much are they worth?

How much money, how much profit will you realize from each of your clients over their "buying lifetime" with you?

This is such an important concept, and I can't emphasize it strongly enough: knowing and understanding this one thing can have a more significant impact on your business than just about anything else you can do.

Once you understand it, a whole new set of factors come into play, and can absolutely revolutionize the way you look at your business, the way you do business, and the profits you'll generate as a result. Let me give you an example to explain what I mean.

Let's say your average sale is $50. Let's say your average client buys from you four times per year.

So from those four transactions, you realize $200 in income. Let's say this client does business with you on average, for ten years. Over those ten years (or their "lifetime" of doing business with you), that average client has been worth $2,000 in income to you.

Now, let's expand this example to a theoretical base of 1,000 clients and see what it means. Those 1,000 clients at $200 a year nets you an annual income of $200,000.

Let's assume that with the proper programs in place, you're able to increase each of the five ways to grow your business we discussed earlier, by only ten percent. Here's what happens:

First, the number of clients you have increased from 1,000 to 1,100.

Next, the average transaction amount per sale increases from $50 to $55.

Third, the average number of purchases per client increases from four times to 4.4 times.

So, the annual income from your client base will increase from $200,000 ($50 x 4 transactions x 1,000 clients) to $266,200 ($55 x 4.4 x 1,100 clients). That's an increase of $66,200 a year!

That's a huge increase!

But if you think that's exciting, wait until you see what happens if you were to extend your client's buying lifetime by just ten percent.

Let's say your clients stay with you for ten years, on average. Your lifetime value from those clients over those ten-years would normally be $2,000,000. But, if you can extend that ten years by just ten percent to 11 years, your total dollar value from these clients will increase from $2,000,000 to $2,928,200 ($266,200 x 11 years)!

An increase of $928,200. Nearly a million dollars! Now, that's a significant increase!

But that's not all. Let's say that you put an effective referral generating system in place, and just ten percent of your 1,000 clients send you a referral with a buying profile the same as your average client.

That's an additional 100 clients who will bring you income of another $266,200 over the 11 years ($55 x 4.4 renewals x 100 clients x 11 years).

Total it all up, and you just made an additional $1,194,400! That's an average of $108,581 per year over the 11 years! Sound impossible? Well, it's not. And it's not all that difficult. It can be done by simply increasing each of the five areas by only ten percent!

Now, how hard would that be to do in your business? Could you realistically, and with some help, increase each of the areas we discussed by ten percent? What about 20 percent?

Some of the businesses, after realizing the power of this key concept and others we've discussed, have increased their businesses by a hundred percent or more in less than a year.

Maybe the numbers and figures I've discussed are realistic for you and your business, and maybe they're not. Perhaps you can't increase each of the areas by the same percentage. That's okay. That doesn't matter.

The point is, you probably have room for improvement in one or more of these areas. If you want your business to be a viable force in the marketplace and give you the lifestyle, the satisfaction, and the income you want, you're going to have to take some proactive steps.

The Value of Your Clients

Without a doubt, knowing the value of your clients influences the way you treat them. As I mentioned before, just knowing how much your clients are worth to you can be invaluable, and can help you in several ways.

We all understand that people don't do business with the same company or business forever. They stop doing business or change whom they do business with for a variety of reasons, and we've already discussed some of those.

But, if you just know, for instance, that your typical client stays with you for say, ten years, on average, and that they're not just a one- or two-time sale, you may begin to treat them differently.

You may treat them with more respect, more kindness, and more courtesy. You may give them some form of special treatment. You may even invite them to special, invitation-only, preferred client programs, or events.

In other words, once you begin to see your clients in a different light, you may begin to do things differently to get them to stay longer as clients.

Next, if you know what the Lifetime Profit Value of your clients is, you'll probably discover you can spend far more to acquire a new client than you originally thought.

In other words, if your average client is worth $2,000 in income to you, you can, theoretically, afford to spend up to $2,000 to bring in a new client and still break even.

In theory, you could spend that $2,000 and still make a profit on the other "back end" products or upsell products or services you might be able to sell them.

If you put an effective referral-generating program in place, you can spend that same $2,000 and make your profits on the referrals they generate.

You and I know it's unrealistic to think you can really afford to spend the full amount of your lifetime income (in this case, $2,000) to get each new client. I'm certainly not suggesting that.

In reality, you can't spend the entire $2,000. You've got to be concerned about things like overhead, cash flow, reserves, and profit. You can't spend money you don't have.

You have to make sure the clients you attract at least match the profile of your average clients, or perhaps are even a little better than average.

There are a several other things you need to

be aware of, as well, such as, "Cost of Acquisition," "Cost of Retention," understanding your margins, and calculating the Marginal Net Worth of your clients.

This book is not the place to go into those in detail; I just bring them to your attention and encourage you to learn about them.

Knowing the Value of Your Clients

Knowing the value of your clients' influences how much you can spend to get a new one, or keep an existing one.

What it really comes down to are two questions: how much can you afford to spend, and how much are you willing to spend, to attract new business?

You may find you can, and are willing to, spend five or six times what your competitors spend. If they're not willing to keep up with you, your business may just explode and leave them in the dust.

Just knowing what your margins are, and that you could spend up to that $2,000 amount and still break even gives you a tremendous edge over your competition.

Here's a real-life example: I have a favorite restaurant I like to go to about twice a month. Meals typically come to about $15. So $15 times 24 meals adds up to $360 in gross sales for the year.

Let's suppose I continue to patronize that restaurant for ten years. That's my buying lifetime with that particular restaurant. That gives the restaurant a total of $3,600 in sales.

If over those ten years I refer ten people, five of whom become regular clients (and that's not very many over ten years), who have spending patterns similar to mine, they'll spend an additional $18,000. (That's five people, times $3,600 a year.)

Add that to the $3,600 I spent, and I've been responsible for generating $21,600 for that restaurant. Even after deducting expenses for overhead, salaries, and food costs, the restaurant still realizes a pretty substantial number of profit dollars from the efforts of pleasing just one person.

Restaurant Example	
A. Amount of average sale	$15
B. Number of sales/year/client (one per month)	12
C. Gross income per year per client (A x B)	$360
D. Number of years client patronizes restaurant	10
E. Gross income over buying lifetime (C x D)	$3,600
F. Number of referrals from client over buying life	10
G. Percent of referrals who become a client	50%
H. Referrals who become clients (G x F)	5
I. Gross income from referrals (E x H)	$18,000
J. Total value of a loyal client (E + I)	$21,600

Now, here's a question: Could that restaurant afford to give away a free meal to attract a new client? Keep in mind I spend $15 a meal, and out of that, about a third of it (or, maybe $5) is profit.

So, the meal really only costs the restaurant $5, and only part of that $5 goes to cover the cost of the food.

The rest of the expense is in overhead, which would have to be paid whether or not a meal was served.

Of course, the answer is yes. They certainly can afford to give away a free meal. Not only that, they can afford to do a number of other things to not only attract new clients, but more importantly, make their existing clients feel more appreciated and special. And you know, when someone feels noticed and important, appreciated, and special, it's just natural they'll want to return.

Let's imagine, for a minute, you are a long-time, faithful client of a certain restaurant. And you brought your family, your clients, and your business associates with you to eat there on a regular basis.

How would you feel if the manager of the restaurant were to offer you and your party a free dessert as a special appreciation gift for your loyalty and for the extra business you brought them? Do you think that little display of appreciation would cause you to want to return again? I think it's pretty safe to say it probably would.

And what about the people who were with you? How do you think they would feel? Do you think they would want to go back to that restaurant? Sure they would. What do you think the restaurant's hard costs of those desserts would be? Do you think the restaurant would lose any money on that gesture?

Well, it's not likely. You see, once you know how much profit your clients are worth to you, long term, then, and only then, can you determine how much you can afford to give away, or to spend, to get new clients, or to keep your existing clients coming back. And you can begin to experiment with different offers to see which ones work best.

Now, here's another thought. Let's say the owner of that restaurant runs an ad, or does a mailing to attract new clients.

And let's say he spends $1,000 for the ad or the mailing, and two couples come in for dinner, and each couple spends $30.

Well, he's taken in a total of $60. But the ad costs were $1,000. So what does he do? What would his competition do?

Does he consider the ad or mail campaign a loser, a total bust, and stop running it? That's what most business people do.

But what about you? What would you do? Well, if you understand the concept of Lifetime Profit Value and Marginal Net Worth, you'll probably think differently.

When you consider the Lifetime Value of those clients and realize that with the proper care and attention, those clients could be responsible for $21,600 each, or $43,200 for the two of them, it changes the picture.

Of course, those numbers are gross revenue figures, and you have to deduct for expenses. And it's over ten years. But, still, that represents a significant amount of money. And all from a $1,000 ad, an ad that most business owners would have given up on.

Now, I'm not suggesting you have to settle for, and be happy with low response rates for your ads. Certainly, you don't. You should always work to improve your ads, your letters, your offers, all your marketing, and give outstanding, compelling reasons and benefits for someone to do business with you.

That's an entire subject, itself, and not the subject of this book. However, we take this subject very seriously, and spend considerable time on it in our workshops and coaching programs.

Let's go back and think about our restaurant example for a minute. Did this idea of stopping an ad just because it didn't break even, or produce a profit for you sound unusual? Different? Strange? Well, maybe to some people, in some businesses.

But, supermarkets and department stores use their own adaptation of this technique all the time. You've probably heard it referred to as a "loss leader."

What they do is advertise a few products at or below cost, to bring new clients into their store, knowing the client will usually buy more products once they're in the store. They also know that unless they get someone to visit their store in the first place, they never stand a chance of making additional or repeat sales, or getting referrals from them these people. Also, since we've already talked about additional and repeat sales to existing clients being generally easier to make, and usually always bring higher profit margins, they understand the ad will pay for itself over the long term.

Just remember this important point:

*The first sale means nothing, unless
you're planning on going out of
business next week. You've got to consider the
Lifetime Profit Value (LPV); what your
client is worth to you over the long haul,
if you really want to be successful.*

Now, what about you, in your business? How can you apply this concept of Lifetime Profit Value?

Well, the first thing you can do is determine your average income per sale. The Lifetime Profit Value "calculator" is provided here for you to use to calculate the Lifetime Profit Value of your own clients, or patients.

Take a few moments to fill in your current figures to get an idea of how much your clients or patients are worth to you.

Understanding not only the concept, but the reality of this exercise, will prove valuable to you, and afford you an insight into your business you may not have thought about before.

The Lifetime Profit Value of Your Clients (Actual)	
A. Amount of average sale	$
B. Number of sales/year/client (one per month)	
C. Gross income per year per client (A x B)	$
D. Number of years client patronizes your business	
E. Gross income over buying lifetime (C x D)	$
F. Number of referrals from client over buying life	
G. Percent of referrals who become a client	%
H. Referrals who become clients (G x F)	
I. Gross income from referrals (E x H)	$
J. Total value of a loyal client (E + I)	$

The next "calculator" is so you may calculate what kind of a difference it will make to your business if you increased each of the areas by ten percent.

Keep in mind, this is a very simplified calculation, yet it is useful for determining your clients' potential value to you.

The Lifetime Profit Value of Your Clients (+10%)	
A. Amount of average sale	$
B. Number of sales/year/client (one per month)	
C. Gross income per year per client (A x B)	$
D. Number of years client patronizes your business	
E. Gross income over buying lifetime (C x D)	$
F. Number of referrals from client over buying life	
G. Percent of referrals who become a client	%
H. Referrals who become clients (G x F)	
I. Gross income from referrals (E x H)	$
J. Total value of a loyal client (E + I)	$

8

What's Next?

Where Do You Go From Here?

Congratulations for making it this far.

You have now been exposed to some of the most powerful and effective techniques, concepts, and ideas available for not only succeeding, but thriving, in business.

No matter how good these ideas are, just being exposed to them is not enough. You must do something with them. For you to get the most value out of this material, you may want to consider developing a step-by-step action plan. An effective and results producing plan should cover these of five areas:

1. Evaluation

Ideas are nothing more than ideas until you put into action. Once acted upon, they have the potential to turn around a struggling business, or help an already successful business become even more dynamic, successful, and profitable.

Before you run out and implement a new

found idea, take the time to evaluate your business as it is now, and determine what areas are most lacking and could use the most attention.

If you will take the time to identify and work on the area of greatest need first, you have the potential of making a significant improvement in your business.

2. Research

Once you've identified your greatest needs and placed them in priority order, you can begin to search out available solutions. Be on an opportunity lookout. The material in this book is just the beginning of the many places you can find good, usable, and practical ideas.

Don't turn any ideas away just because you think they might not pertain to your business or the way you operate. Capture them and apply step number three.

3. Personalization

As you encounter new ideas, keep an open mind. Study them. Analyze them. Think them through. Ask yourself if an application can be made to your specific situation by simply changing or modifying part of the concept or idea.

If a specific illustration uses a type of product

or service that you don't sell for the example, a simple adjustment might be all that's needed.

Create a written plan of action and begin to organize your thoughts, first, as to what you intend to implement. Organize your current database and make the mental and written commitment to yourself that you are going to improve your skill sets and be more creative in client outreach. If you don't have your clients in a database, this is the time to create one. You may wish to order new personalized business cards or new stationery. Begin collecting testimonials from clients immediately; never let that opportunity pass you by. If you haven't been a gift-giver to clients who make major purchases, now is the time to begin.

The book is designed to motivate you and offer you ideas you can implement. We cover a lot more in our workshops.

4. Implementation

You know, membership in a health club won't do you any good unless you go to the club and participate in the exercise program. It is the same with the information in this book.

It's of no practical use unless you implement it. It's easy to come up with good ideas and develop plans, but where most people get bogged down is when it comes to putting them into action. It's not always easy, but if you're going to truly be successful, you must do whatever it takes to act on your plans.

5. Review

After you've worked with your new ideas for a while, stop and evaluate how things are working. You may need to make some adjustments so you can continue to see improvement.

Sometimes, an idea you thought was great doesn't work out at all. That's okay, don't continue using it. Just scrap it and move on to something else. Next!

On the other hand, if you find an idea that works well, see if you can refine it, or "plus" it, to make it even more effective.

That's all there is to it. It sounds simple enough to say, but in reality, there's a lot to do. The plain and truthful facts are most people simply won't take the time and effort to do the things we've just discussed. Heck, many people who purchase this book will never even read it! That's unfortunate, because they could be even more successful than they are now if they did.

The good news is, their failure to take action is

good for you. Because if it's you who does these things, it will be you who realizes the success.

You now have the tools . . .

GO FOR IT!

About the Author

Dr. Richard Kaye received his Bachelor of Science Degree in business, from Long Island University, in 1973. He went on to receive his Doctorate of Chiropractic from the Columbia Institute of Chiropractic in New York in 1976. After 30-years in private practice in San Diego, California, he retired to pursue the entrepreneurial life.

Prior to entering the field of health care, he was an electronics engineer working in the field of communications. His distinguished career includes being named Outstanding Doctor of the Year, as well as Doctor of The Year, by the San Diego County Chiropractic Society.

He served as President of the San Diego County Chiropractic Society from 1981 through 1983, and was Chairman of the Board of Directors of the Sacro Occipital Research Society, International (SORSI), from 1986 through 1988. Dr. Kaye was a founding member of the Board of Directors of The Association for Network Care, in 1994. In addition to having appeared on numerous television and radio shows, he has authored many published articles.

Dr. Kaye is an internally acclaimed lecturer, having presented seminars and workshops in Australia, France, Japan, and Russia, as well as in the United States.

Richard sat on the Advisory Board of Brian

Anderson Entertainment. He served as an Advisory Board Member for Pacific Rim Institute for Development and Education (PRIDE), a Non-Governmental Organization (NGO) member of the United Nations, and Excellerated Enterprises, a multi-national teaching organization. He served as Vice President of Investor Relations for RacelandUSA, LLC (a 1,140 acre motocross complex in the desert, east of San Diego).

Dr. Kaye served as a Board Member for the Enchanted Circle (Taos, New Mexico) Sirolli Institute. He is a member of the Board of Directors of the Taos Entrepreneurial Network. He was a member of the board of directors of the Global Gateway Community, and was Secretary of the Board of Directors for Style for Life. He is a faculty member of CEO Space (a multi-national business growth organization).

He is also a member of the Board of Directors of the Integrative Medicine de Taos organization.

Richard has been featured on KGTV in San Diego, as well as on KTLA television, Los Angeles, California, on several occasions, discussing two of his specialties: Team Building and Super Networking. He was also featured on PBS; an in-depth story about the leading-edge health-care he practiced.

At the Chopra Center, in La Costa, California, where he shared the platform with Lisa Nichols (star of *The Secret*, *The Larry King Live Show*, and *The Oprah Winfrey Show*) he spoke about:

Consciousness, Cooperation, and Contribution – thriving in the developing recession.

He's presented *The Secrets of Empowering Negotiation* for Peak Potentials Training, Master of Influence program.

Richard was one of three consultants to the Peak Potentials Coaching Program, Peak State of Mind.

He speaks around the nation about the Secrets of Empowering Negotiation.

Richard resides in Taos, New Mexico.

For additional information about Dr. Kaye, the the programs he teaches and how you can increase your bottom-line and take better financial care of yourself and your family, and how you can book him to facilitate trainings about *The Secrets of Empowering Negotiation*, for your company, group, or organization, go to . . .

richardkaye.com

Index

A

B

C

D

H

I

J

K

L

M

Y

Z

www.ingramcontent.com/pod-product-compliance
Lightning Source LLC
Chambersburg PA
CBHW031508270326
41930CB00006B/305